UBER TALES

with Rule-Based System
for Making Money

By Anatoly Bilenko

Philadelphia, USA

2018

Cover Design by Anatoly Bilenko

Available from Amazon.com and other retail outlets

For My Family

CONTENTS

Contents

Introduction

This book explains my systematic approach to driving for ride-sharing company like Uber or Lyft. I don't go into intricacies of Uber app, its many uses and options, because I find it unnecessary to re-hash Uber's own manual. I read entire driver's side of Uber's website in about 2 hours (I was taking notes) – it's the best training session I have ever seen. This online manual teaches everything there is to know about app, rules and regulations, rights and responsibilities... and then it tells you "go driving". My book picks up where they left off by describing WHAT to drive, WHERE to go, WHEN to do it, HOW to manage, and WHY or WHY NOT, with a list of Rules to follow.

Kamikaze Express

On Monday afternoon, I was running some errands in town and decided to take Uber Pool Express for a quick $4 ride. Express is a tricky class – the pickup is on a corner – often dangerous for the driver or inconvenient for a rider. I always struggle with these, as a driver. If I stop on a busy road, I risk being rear-ended by other cars. If I turn a corner, or pull into nearest parking lot – it's a nuisance for the client. If there is no place on a corner to stand (typical situation in suburbs and countryside)… you get my drift. I really wanted to see how another driver deals with it and how it looks from the client's point of view.

I was standing exactly at a pick up spot shown in the rider's app. Car came up on the opposite side of the road. Why did app send me to this corner and not across the road, so I would stand on a side where my car is coming on? Things went downhill from that point on. Driver actually was attempting to make left, across four lanes, in afternoon traffic…like some kamikaze. I started to cartoonishly signal with my hands.

Signal 1 – stupid.

Signal 2 – make a right.

Signal 3 – wait there.

Frustrated after waiting for 10 minutes and perspired from running across major road in 90 degrees heat, I was glad to finally find respite in leather cavern of Toyota Rav4… except it was the same 90, no AC and all windows were down. "Mother fucker", no, I didn't say it, but I thought it very expressively. No water, no candy, but a pile of his own shit on a passenger front seat. Obviously, he never heard of Rule #2.

I looked around a car. Brand new 2018, premium package, AWD – he made every mistake possible. His phone was down by cup holders, so he had to look down to see map and directions. "Why not put the phone into some heavy duty mount in a middle of dashboard, straight and plumb, as instructed by Uber? Why put yourself into unsafe conditions, by constantly looking down and away from the road?" no, I didn't say it, but I thought it breathing heavily. He doesn't know about Rule #1.

"So, how do you like driving for Uber?" - I asked a standard question. He exploded: "I've been driving twelve weeks and it's no good. Gas is too much, my car costs too much, I'm not making enough and I can feel this car breaking. I can feel my brand new car falling apart!" Man was devastated.

I wish this book was finished earlier - I would give him a copy for free - THEN, he would find out about Rule #5.

Don't be that guy.

Follow the simple Rule-based system – the only way to do the right thing, in the right place, at the right time – ALL THE TIME!

I illustrate my Rules on the pages of this book as best as I can, with reasoning and colorful examples betwixt UBER TALES.

OFFER

I don't share my knowledge for free, but there is a way to make it cost you nothing.

If you sign up to drive for Uber or Lyft, using my codes, and complete required amount of rides – I will receive a bonus. It doesn't come out from your pocket. Company pays for promotion and enticing a new driver to join. If you sign up with my code, I will see your progress in app and will be able to keep in touch. Once I receive a bonus, I will put $20 in an envelope and mail it to you, making this book – absolutely FREE!

UBER   ANATOLYB66UE

LYFT   ANATOLY57387

May all your rides be smooth.

Maiden Voyage

I've been looking at this beautiful white thing,
thinking how in the world am I going to keep it clean and
without damage. Long days under the sun and many
hours of labor will eventually take its toll, there will be
nicks and scratches, people will surely destroy the
interior, but for now – it's a shiny and clean Beloye Taksi
– The White Cab.

On Wednesday, registration finally came in and I
immediately signed it up into my Uber account.
Paperwork was approved by the time I put water bottles
and candy in. Adjustment of the driver seat thou… that
took the rest of the afternoon. I wasn't rushing –
everything has to be set up just right – Uber iPhone, my
navigation, phone, stylus, my candy, water. I mean, I
have to live inside this small space for many hours, it has
to be both comfortable and functional.

Then comes the test. I went out around 6pm for
few hours to get used to new car and its contraptions. I
went for usual spots and… nothing. Not a single ping.
Two hours later I knew something is wrong, but couldn't
figure out the source of the problem until alert came in
without the sound. Bingo! Uber iPhone wants to play

thru the car speakers. I didn't figure it out, it was two teenage girls I picked up from that silent ping.

After I managed to rectify the sound situation things started cooking. Beloye Taksi got a steady stream of 10 to 20 minute rides – just what I wanted. Right away there were compliments about how nice it looks and clean smell and all that. First run had been going swimmingly and I kept on rolling.

12:45am call comes in from some bumblefuck fifteen minutes away. Although not far from small towns, that place is legit in the middle of some forest, with one lane road not wide enough for two cars to pass, and no shoulder (just a big-ass ditch). I found the place all right, but decided not to drive up the driveway, because the house is way deeper into the forest. I can see light in a couple of windows, but nothing else. Nobody is coming.

Five minutes passes and I am starting to get a bad juju, so I call 'em up like "Hi, I'm your Uber, I don't know if I'm at the right place. Can you see my car outside?" (Meaning, "yo, I been sitting here outside chilling my bones. Harry up, beAch, the meter is running.") My worst fears realized – drunk woman with trembling voice, whispering: "Don't come up the driveway, wait on a road, turn headlights off and keep the motor running".

Shiiit. What have I got myself into?

After few more minutes I decided that:

a.   It's stupid.

b.   I am in a deep completely dark forest.

c.   I am the captain of this ship and I get to decide what goes on and off and where.

So I put light back on, got my flash-light and stepped outside to meet my passenger. She was in dark knee-high pajamas and army-type boots, hair sticking every which way, no makeup. Suitcase. I offer to put it in a trunk. The thing feels almost empty.

We actually had a nice talk about Russian literature and music. She had Vysotsky* on her phone and we listened to "Wolf Hunt". She explained that although she doesn't understand the words, she can feel the "haunting power of the song". Her words. Imagine her shock when I offered a translation about surrounded wolf and hunters and dogs, and breaking out from obedience…

She was running away from husband number 2 or number 3 (she kept mixing them up). I learned a lot on that hour-long drive to a … parking lot on a shopping mall. The fuck? She actually spoke to a guy waiting there for some time. She was afraid he would leave, so she kept telling him how close we are. "Only few minutes away. O, you so nice to me. I'm so glad I have you" and more and more like this.

I don't know what the story with the future husband number 4 is, but he was definitely losing patience and even asked her if she is lying. Finally, we arrived at that Walmart and she jumped out as soon as Beloye Taksi stopped. As I was handing her the bag, she was on a phone and kept saying that she is waiting for him in a store and cannot see him anywhere.

Walmart was closed. She WAS lying.

---

*Vladimir Vysotsky was a famous Russian singer/songwriter in 1970's. During his relatively short career, Vysotsky enjoyed unparalleled success in Soviet Union - on a level of Beatles in Western world. Many of his songs had deeply emotional and humanistic depiction of some of the most dramatic periods of Russian history (revolution, Stalin's repressions, WWII, etc.), as well as minstrel repertoire of love and loss ballads, friendship and courtship, and current events. His songs about alpine climbers are absolutely my favorites – I can recite them all by heart. Vysotsky's lyrics had deeply anti-Soviet undertones, often disguised as humor and satire.

His music career was largely stifled by lifelong KGB surveillance, so much so that only few official recordings of Vysotsky exist, despite the fact that he has given hundreds of concerts. These 'slightly' illegal concerts were organized on a shoestring at college auditoriums, community theatres and culture clubs. Tickets would sell out within hours, without any advertisement, just by the word of mouth. Many attendees would bring their own audio-reel recorders – heavy suitcase size monstrosities with tape on two reels, thick wires and rudimentary microphone (this is before CD, before audio tape, before 8-track). It was customary to be dead quiet at those concerts (even applause were shunned), so the bootleg recordings don't get screwed up. My dad had 5 or 6 of those 'slightly' illegal reels.

Vysotsky had lustrous actor career, with leading role in major popular movie where he portrays a hero cop (think a mix of Bruce Willis with Russell Crowe and a pinch of Harvey Keitel); and his famous depiction of Shakespeare Hamlet on stage, that considered iconic in Russian theatre and widely emulated to this day. Vysotsky was married to French woman (which was unheard of in Soviet Union), lived abroad at times and gave a series of sold-out concerts to Anglo-French audience... in Russian language.

He was an alcoholic and drug addict, and died at the age of 42. Although no official announcement of his death were made, he lied for 3 days in improvised repose at the theatre where he worked, with continuous attendance of over 100,000 people daily. On a day of the funeral, crowd was 9km deep and flowers were sold out in entire Moscow city. Reportedly, it was the third largest funeral in Soviet history, only behind of Lenin and Stalin. Such was the affection of the nation for its beloved bard.

Chapter 1

Don't be a Fake Bitch

One of the most important decisions for a full time Uber driver is what kind of car to drive. Let me be absolutely clear: any car will do as long as it's a 4-door, not a truck, not a box van. Passenger car, SUV or mini-van – you can be on a road tomorrow, but if you are like me (and treat this gig as a business) then you need to buy an appropriate vehicle.

Black

The word around campfire is that Uber driver got to have a full size SUV like Chevy Suburban, big Cadillac or Lincoln, or Toyota Sequoia, all black of course inside and out. The thought process seems to make sense: these big boys qualify for all classes – Pool, X, SUV, LX and Black, so there will be more work for it. However, there are several concerns.

First of all, I am not sure how much "Black" work is out there. Maybe New-York, LA or London have plenty of crazy rich people who don't care about the costs, but here (in the average America) those are few and far between. I drive rich people all the time – they are perfectly fine with "X". When I ask if they have taken "Black" before, the most common answer is "we needed a large car, because there where 5 (or 6) of us". Few said that they wanted to "arrive in style" and "company was paying for it". Some guy admitted that he tried to impress girls with "Black" and it didn't work... Not very encouraging, in my opinion.

Secondly, I am pretty sure that since most work is for "Pool" and "X", you will end up giving $3.50 rides in $60,000 (or more) automobile, burning 12-16 miles per gallon (mpg) of gas. Big SUV is the least fuel efficient of all, driving a largest cost of your business even higher... all in hopes to pick up that mythical whale ready to splurge a hundred bucks on a twenty dollar ride. These big boys are very expensive to buy and even more costly to maintain. Hell, a set of tires can set you back a thousand dollars (and those are cheap ones).

Finally, these cars are really, REALLY BIG. So much so, I saw them scraping parked cars on downtown streets, I saw them driving partially on a side walk with two wheels on a curb on narrow roads of Manayunk, I saw them totally unable to navigate thru tiny alleys of West Chester. It is a complete nightmare for those drivers.

XL

As you can guess, dear reader, I have never driven "Black" and have no plans to start. I do have a personal experience with "XL", i.e. large mini-Van like

Honda Odyssey or Toyota Sienna. There are several advantages and drawbacks I can attest to personally.

Clearly, "XL" is the next most popular option behind "X" and "Pool" and rightfully so as it is most convenient for a large group as well as travelers with a lot of luggage, or very tall people who "like to stretch out" (don't laugh, I had one of those). Unfortunately, these types of rides happen infrequently and mostly on weekends. They are fun. People go to and from weddings and corporate events, all festive and in good mood. A bunch of friends go to a concert or 'pre-game', blasting energetic music thru my aux-cord. A big family going to a weekend getaway… to their friend's mansion down Jersey Shore. All very enjoyable, but this "fun" doesn't come free – you will always spend time waiting, because they are never ready on time all together, because you need to load and unload, because somebody always needs to make a stop along the way and on and on. And then weekend ends, and it all goes away. Back to "X" and "Pool", and Uber just loves these vans for Pool, especially in the city where they can keep throwing additional legs for hours on end.

I had a particular difficulty with the type of van I drove – an older Honda Odyssey with manual doors. People got used to newer models with automatic doors and got a habit of just standing in front of side-door, waiting for it to open. Seeing what's going on I resorted to jumping out in order to open the door for numbnuts. Then I got a great fear of this heavy door rolling back, breaking fingers and toes of slow-settling passengers (it's a serious liability and a major risk to avoid) – so I started to jump out every time to at least close the door for them. All this running around was catching up with me pretty quick, plus it was dangerous too, as I often had to step out into incoming traffic. I strongly recommend to get an automatic door option if you want to go "XL" route.

These Vans are almost as wide as big Black SUV's, so they pose similar problems on narrow city streets. Fuel economy will be better with 6 cylinder 3 liter engines versus 5 liter V8 in big SUV. I was squeezing 20-22 mpg out of Odyssey in mixed road driving, but only 16-18 mpg with both AC units running on a hot summer day. Frankly, I think it's too much. Had there be an affordable Van in slightly smaller size with more efficient engine, I would go for it, but I couldn't find one.

It would take a book bigger than this just to go through all possible combinations of body and engine and amenities of great variety of vehicles on a road today, so it is not my intention. Rather, I want to illustrate thought process that has to go into choosing the car you are going to spend thousands of hours in and spend thousands of dollars on. The kind of vehicle you choose has to be based not only on a class of service you want to provide, but also may highly depend on your local weather conditions. This brings me to mid-size 4x4 SUV, like Toyota Highlander or Ford Explorer and their smaller cousins.

SUV

Up North, where winters are long and snowy, all-wheel drive is a must. If safety of your riders and yourself is an absolute priority (and Rule # 1), then you have to get a vehicle capable of handling slippery and low traction weather conditions. Otherwise you are out of work for months which, depending on volume of moonshine you produce, may not be such a bad idea... he-he.

I live sort of in a middle of America, around 40th parallel. Here we don't have severe winters except couple of snow storms and occasional sleet and freezing rain. Prices for rides surge to upside like crazy during these periodic squalls. Philly and most surrounding suburbs are flaming red on an app screen, with prices 3-4 times multiple of the usual rate. Indeed, these snowmaggedon surges can reach absolutely crazy, astronomical levels. This, dear reader, is an epitome of free markets – a supply and demand forces in a battle for monetary equilibrium.

In other words: every driver with even a tiny bit of sense and healthy instinct of self-preservation went home. There is got to be a point when you say: "Hey, this is not worth me wrecking my car and risking myself and my passengers". As amount of active Ubers decrease, people start literally betting for cars until prices reach levels where riders decide that "it's too much money, maybe I should wait it out instead". Clients pull back and prices stabilize. At this point in time only people who "must go no matter what" will pay highly elevated price for whatever limited number of 4x4 SUV's are still on a road. Importantly, they mostly understand the risks and will go for SUV-class almost exclusively.

I want to point out that driving 4x4 is not a panacea against accidents. First of all, they skid just like the rest, even worse considering that "steer towards the skid" is ineffective for all-wheel drive vehicles. I have seen them lose traction, spin out of control and get into horrible accidents because the driver became overly confident, was driving too fast or underestimated braking distance. Secondly, you are not alone on a road, with other drivers who may be poorly equipped or not experienced enough. They are the ones who will skid on an icy patch through the intersection and crash into you – YOU, perfectly standing still in your super-safe SUV. Now, you are out of work for weeks while your car is being repaired, in addition to an out-of-pocket deductible and headaches with insurance.

So my advice with choosing a car for Uber is simply this: "Don't be a fake bitch" (my daughter once told me that – I nearly drove off the road). Don't just get a flashy big car to impress your former co-workers. Don't take excessive risks in poor weather to earn bragging rights for your barbeque get-together. Instead think rationally and objectively about typical weather where you live and your personal risk tolerance. Also think about added costs. SUV's are not fuel efficient, because it takes more gas to run front and rear wheels together as well as pull along a much heavier vehicle. They are also quite expensive. And, of course, there is always an option to move south of 40th parallel, were winter weather is simply not a factor. LOL.

Choosing a Car

A good rule of thumb is to look what kind of cars is common among taxi-cabs and livery car services in your area. This is exactly how I zeroed in on my Toyota Camry. Four door sedans are generally a very good choice for transportation – a basic passenger car, easy and convenient to drive, fuel efficient and reasonable to maintain, with many different makes and models to choose from. The word around my mechanic's garage is that Japanese cars are more reliable and that my Toyota will run 300,000 miles (the jury is still out on that), but I want to point out that origin of the car is a moot point in today's auto industry. To wit, my car is made by Toyota of Northern Kentucky and assembled on Subaru plant in Indiana… this is not your pop's car world.

American Made

It reminds me of a feud I had with Gary, angry neighbor of mine, around the time President George W. Bush tried to re-introduce "Buy American" mantra. Gary was fuming about filthy immigrants buying Jap cars instead of good 'ol Murican automobiles.

To illustrate my point I had to take him to a little sticker located on a pillar of a driver side door. There, he was shocked to find out that his Caddy and Ford are really made in Canada and Mexico, while my Honda and Mazda were assembled in Alabama and Missouri. Gary was so upset, he took off his "Buy American" bumper sticker and didn't talk to me for about a year, which I actually enjoyed quite a bit.

There are several important features to look for when choosing a car.

1. It has to fit you personally. Take a test drive, see how you like it. Are you comfortable? Do you like the ride?

2. Go on a back seat, where most of your riders will sit. Is it comfortable? Does it have ample amount of leg room? Check out shoulder room (this and other information is available from manufacturer website, your dealer or third-party sites like Edmunds.com, etc.). An average person is a bit over 18 inches wide, so look for a car with no less than 54 inches of interior width, i.e. shoulder and hip room, for 3 riders to fit comfortably in the back.

3. It has to be powerful enough to pull a car full of people uphill, but not too much, otherwise it's a waste of gas. I opted for the biggest of small engines: 2.5 Liter 4-Cylinder. It does the job well.

4. Your car has to be a popular, mass-produced model. This will make spare parts more accessible and affordable. It will also be familiar to your mechanic – they probably seen all your future problems before and practiced on somebody else's car.
5. The price must be right.

Natural inclination for most people who consulted me about buying a car for Uber is to either lease a new car or buy old one cheaply. Both ways are wrong, but leasing is outright dangerous to your financial health. Leasing agreement has a predetermined maximum allowed annual mileage of typically 12,000 miles. There are variations, with 16K being the highest of what I saw. May be there are bigger leases out there, but this is not enough for Uber, as full time driver will do 30-50K per year or more, depending on your local situation. Naturally, your dealer will assure you that you can return your car at the end of the lease back to him, in this dealership, not to get charged any extra and just switch to a new one. Bullshit! These car salesmen are lying snakes by design. They were taught to deceive and mislead customers as a sales technique.

The Tie Guy

I actually had a personal experience with this when I was looking for a side-gig many years ago. I wanted to do something commission based with flexible schedule, as I am a good salesman and can sell you the Brooklyn Bridge on a bright sunny day. My choice seemed to be between real estate and auto dealership. Since I knew a whole lot more about cars than houses, I entered a training program with major company in Philadelphia area. They had multiple locations, selling hundreds of cars every day and needed young energetic people to join their team… and blah-blah-blah.

I was utterly perplexed when our "teacher", pink-colored gentleman with $100 tie, proceeded to list the most sleaziest and dishonest ways to "sell this crap to marks". Myriad of different approaches to bamboozle people was all he talked about. When I asked: "Are we going to learn anything about the product we actually have to sell – the CARS, you 'no?" He answered: "This is not a part of this training program", and looked kind of funky at me.

On a second day, the guy-with-$100-tie was focused on compensation – a cobweb of schemes, upsells and rebates. How many of what kind of cars to sell for highest commissions on a sliding scale… He was going for hours, writing columns on a whiteboard, all percents and fractions and no mention of actual price. So I asked: "There are prices of these cars, clearly stated on a window sticker. Isn't it the selling price? If it is not, then maybe you can tell me the correct amount and I go sell them… No?" Pinkish gentlemen turned a shade of violet and hissed back: "May be you are not a right person for this job?"

On a third day they didn't let me into training facility, because "program is full and you've been bumped". The rest of those guys are the salesmen you meet at your local dealership. Beware!

The correct way to buy a car for Uber is NOT to get carried away. Car payment will be the largest single bill to pay in this business, so a fine balance needs to be found between cost and quality. The first step in reducing cost is NOT to buy a new car, but find one 2 or 3 years old and finance it 4-5 years out. You are looking for a car that comes off somebody's lease with low mileage and minimum wear. The kind of a car some guy drove to work 10 miles away or an elderly couple used to run errands around town. (Hint: Go to suburban dealership) Now their 2-3 year lease is up, and they return it back to dealership, and in perfect condition so not to get screwed with extra charges. You are looking for a car that was sold and serviced at that dealership and ask to see maintenance records. They keep everything on a computer these days. If the car was really serviced as prescribed with no major repairs, then they should be able to produce the proof. Otherwise, look around, maybe guy with-$100-tie is lurking in shadow nearby... you 'no.

The huge cost advantage of buying a slightly used car is that you avoid that drop in price – a significant loss of value when a new car goes off the lot. This cliff-drop in price is a result of the car ceasing to be new and can be

20-30% of original price in the first year alone. After that value of the car slides gradually until it becomes an old clunker and practically worthless. A little maneuver of getting 2-3 year old car allows a savvy buyer to enjoy most of value and usability without paying top dollar for it.

This almost new car out of the lease has to be financed to buy for 4-5 years. Low financing rates are widely available even with low credit score or without credit history. If you want to buy a car, THEY will find a way to do it. The trick is to keep monthly payments around $300 for an Uber X-class sedan. I will explain this number in chapter on *Money*, with usual proviso that this is an average amount. Your mileage may vary, as they say. If in doubt or have choices, go for the one that costs less – to build a margin of safety into your business. You will live with this payment for 5 long years, so consider it carefully, don't get carried away and always err on a side of caution.

At the end of 4 -5 years of payments you will have a fully paid off 6 to 8 years old car, that can hopefully be used for a couple more years. Now you get to drive it for free, or plan ahead and start saving some money for down payment on your next bigger and blacker SupaUBA. Remember that Uber limits an age of its fleet to 10 years (12 for hybrids), which brings me back to common misconception of buying an "old and cheap" car. Don't do it! Be smart for your business, be a seller of old car and not a buyer. Just like in stock market, you have to buy low and sell high. Buy low mileage, sell high mileage – then you make money. Do it the other way around and you will lose. Don't lose money!

I would be remiss not to mention hybrid cars, represented by Toyota Prius in its many iterations. This car is unparalleled in fuel efficiency and notorious for reliability and low maintenance cost. I actually wanted to buy Prius, but all the used ones had hundreds of thousand miles on them (I know exactly what they've been doing with those Priuses...he-he). This particular car has a certain stigma of been called "Pussy Wagon" and "Fag-Mobile", probably due to original advertisements targeting sensitive females and environmentally-conscientious yuppies as the type to drive Prius. Despite publicity that hurt the brand, these cars gain popularity among cab drivers. The highest rated Uber driver I ever met was driving Prius with over 200K on it. Hybrid cars, especially Prius, have to be a major consideration. Just don't be a fake bitch about it.

Maintenance

The wonderful plan I laid out (of buying a slightly used car and driving it for many years) has a serious problem. High mileage and wear will undoubtedly take its toll and require constant attention as well as some planning. To make sure that my car can run for 300,000 miles or more I take special care of routine maintenance and operation.

1. I use only high quality gasoline. Any car will run its best on 92-94 octane gas. I can hear the difference in more even tone of pistons at idle and absents of engine nock when I accelerate sharply. The difference in performance is indisputable, thou it comes at a price. High grade gasoline can be 30% more expensive than Regular, but don't be alarmed. It's not a problem with most cars, because engine runs more efficiently on Super and actually uses 10-20% less gas, thus mitigating some of the costs.

You can calculate this difference for your specific car quite precisely by recording how many gallons you pump and amount of miles driven. Just don't take a single day as an indicator. Instead, make records over prolong period of 1-2 weeks to ensure that it covers all types of driving (fuel efficiency is higher on a highway and lower in a city). Make sure to start with nearly empty tank of gas and finish about the same. Divide total miles driven by total volume of gallons of gas. Do these records for Regular (87) and Super (93) and compare the results. (Note: You don't have to test mid-range gas. It's just a mix of the other two.) To ensure fairness of the test, try to conduct it when weather is about the same, because fuel efficiency drops significantly when air-conditioner is on and also suffers a bit with heater-defroster.

Every single car of mine I ever tested showed marked improvement in miles driven per gallon on 93-Octane gasoline (92 and 94 will be about the same, but not as widely available). The increase in fuel efficiency was in a range of 10-30%, with largest improvement for biggest engine (I drove 5L V8 Dodge Ram for many years), and smallest difference for tiny 4-Cylinder Hyundai (that car was something else entirely).

Alongside of practically not costing any extra, 93 gas burns the cleanest in an engine. Contrary to some advertisements, it doesn't actually "clean" anything inside an engine. It just doesn't leave as much gunk, helping pistons work like new for many years.

Not all gasoline is created equal. I strongly believe that there is a significant difference in quality of gas offered by major oil companies and some unbranded odd gas stations without steady supply. Exxon/Mobil, Chevron/Texaco, Shell, BP and Sunoco are some of widely available brand name producers, selling highest quality gasoline from their own refineries. This stuff will be the freshest, cleanest, best-burning gasoline – the ONLY food for my Beloye Taksi (the White Cab). The left-overs, old stock and refinery batches of inferior chemical quality will be sold to second tier wholesalers and then to off-brand gas stations. So, it's not always bad. Sometimes it is an OK gas for less money, but you truly don't know what you are getting. These second tier suppliers are notorious for mixing tainted gasoline with other inappropriate liquids. People periodically go to jail for this, but a new crook always seems to replace the old one. In New-York these gas stations are called warmly: "The Worst Horse Piss". Think about it.

2. I extend the same approach used for gasoline to engine oil. Changing oil and filter must be done at regular intervals to ensure proper engine operation. I check oil weekly to add if necessary and to make sure it doesn't look too dark or smells burnt, but I rarely have this problem because I use only Synthetic oil. Full synthetic, not blend, and stick to big names (Mobil is my favorite). On a top of a fact that Synthetic oil actually works better, it also lasts longer. Full Synthetic can be used for 6-10K miles between changes, with 15K Mobil available and I am sure more to come. Yes, it costs more to buy than conventional oil, but it keeps working 2-3 times longer. This is truly a case of "Stingy Pays Twice", because using Synthetic oil really costs less, while also minimizing trips to mechanic and saving time.

3. The same logic has to be applied to other maintenance issues, including repair. Pick better parts, quality brakes, bigger batteries, etc. If you want your car to run like new – use factory parts – the ones it had when it was new. There is no doubt that quality pays for itself, but there is an important caveat. When the car gets older, towards the end of its 8-10 years of useful life (for Uber at least) and with high mileage, these repair situations need to be taken on case-by-case basis. For example, I would question the need for top-of-the-line 80K tires, when car is 9 years old, has 350K miles on it and in constant need of repairs. It may simply not last that long.

Think for yourself!

Beloye Taksi

My car is a Toyota Camry 2015 LE.
White, no window tint.
2.5 Liter, 4-Cylinder engine.

Average fuel consumption – 29 mpg on Sunoco 93
in mixed driving over wide range of weather. Summer
averages 25-26 mpg, but in mild weather I easily do 31-34
mpg. Long highway trips clock at over 40 mpg (nice!).
I love to drive it, it is very comfortable and spacious for
driver and passengers, with ample leg room and wide
enough for three adults to sit snugly. Once I had 5 people
in the back seat (they were college students – skinny and
drunk). I had it fully loaded with 4 passengers and
tightly packed trunk of luggage on many occasions.
Handling was fine and engine had plenty of power to go
uphill without engine knock (on 93 Sunoco). I bought it
2 years old out of lease with very low sub-20K mileage. It
still had original tires and back seat looked like it was
never used at all. Maintenance records at dealership had
nothing except oil changes at regular intervals. Perfect!

I don't know how I didn't notice it during test
drive (maybe because my dealer just wouldn't shut up),
but interior of this car rattles like a cheap Chinese toy.
I mean every single plastic part in it screeches, squeaks or
cracks all the time. Front seats thumping in their
assemblies, seat belt buckles banging into plastic door
pillars – a cacophony of noises dislodged by every bump
in a road. It was so bad, I actually cut rubber bands into

pieces and stuffed them into every seam in the interior, using small flathead screwdriver, to create sort of a gasket in-between plastic paneling. After many attempts I managed to rectify most noises, except a particularly nasty screech coming from where passenger side dashboard rubs against LCD display and control panel. Two pieces didn't fit together at all, with noticeable gap about half way down. One day I got so frustrated with squeaky-rubby sounds, I took a toothpick out of my mouth and stuck it in-between, about 1 inch above the gap... the noise stopped. It's still there – a broken off piece of toothpick. I am afraid to touch it and take special care to clean around it when I wipe off the dashboard. I thought I looked when I was buying it, but somehow I didn't see that floor carpeting doesn't fit this car properly. Although nothing major is fundamentally affected, I am kinda queasy about design and build of this marvel of Japanese engineering, assembled in Indiana and stuffed tight with premium toothpicks and high quality rubber bands. To date it didn't give me any mechanical problems outside of usual maintenance like brakes, tires, etc.

So yea, I overpaid for it a little, but it's not like I had many choices. There were only a couple of these. I could have gone with older/cheaper version, but this 2015 Toyota already had rear-view camera. I was ready to pay extra for this feature and was proved right. Rearview camera is great help in tight turnarounds, allows more precision and quite literally saved my behind on several occasions. There were better deals on other colors, but I was locked into White. Everything pointed to this Camry, that was a little more higher priced, because it also had a special $600 security feature installed.

Payments came out to a bit under $320/month and I was fine with it, except I was looking to see what added security I had and how to use it, but could not find it anywhere. So I stopped by their service department, where an All-Pink-Guy didn't listen to me very carefully and just kept repeating slower and louder (so a dumb no-speak-English immigrant can understand): " It's A Spe-ci-al Se-cu-ri-ty Fea-ture." I understand, I will never get that $600 back. I'm not stupid and yes, I speak English, but I ain't no fake bitch either. So, at least in this book, I'm gonna tell how it is.

Marshall

Just before noon on Thursday, I picked up a passenger going to the Airport. Guy looked sharp in a dark blue suit, tie was already off. Kid didn't seem to be a year over 35, but I bet that at 45 he will look just the same. The only piece of luggage is a backpack. Nice shoes. He promptly revealed that he arrived late last night from Atlanta (freak rain-storm delayed his flight), had two meetings ending with lunch at Chinese restaurant and now was heading back home.

He spoke slowly.

I swear I could smell MSG on his breath and that rotten stench of a restaurant kitchen oozing from his clothes. Chinese crap didn't agree with his stomach. Guy was skillfully suppressing the burps, but the odor was impossible to conceal. As he was opening and closing the window, with air-conditioner of Beloye Taksi blasting on '5', I took mercy on him and offered my last bottle of water.

That did the trick.

Relieved and now relaxed, the man proceeded to tell his life story, with only rudimentary prodding required on my part. As it turned out, kid was born in Southern Georgia near Florida border. Not a surprise that he finds Philadelphia 'a little bizarre', but still wants to bring his children for a visit to the City of Brotherly Love - see the Liberty Bell, take a tour on a Red Bus, ... the works. (Only later I realized that it must be for him akin to me taking my own kids to the Zoo. To see animals in their own habitat, you 'no...) I made an observation that people Down South are a lot different from us here in PA and NY, but didn't indicate how. To my surprise, he didn't dig in, but instead replied in a beautiful Southern Drawl how his business takes him all over the country and : "Only Down South can I speak like at home..."

A Pause.

Our eyes met in a rear-view mirror. Southern Gentleman had clear eyes. Not the color. The expression. Searching, looking, laughing, reading like an X-Ray. The eyes with intellect, reason and calm. Rarest thing ever.

I know.

Just to be sure, the blue-suit-man started a half-assed effort to classify Carolina's and Maryland as a sort of mixed border line, but I wouldn't have any of it. I already SAW him. Just one mention of Mason-Dixon Line (with all its Civil War baggage) removed all remaining guard-fences of a Georgian farmer's youngest son.

That's what he was.

When Father got too old and wanted to rest (his word - not 'retire' - 'REST'), two brothers concocted a plan how to get some money out of the farm quick, but still keep most of the land. They actually subdivided some of their territory and sold lots for houses to be built on. This, my friends, is a pure genius - land to build is the most profitable slice of Real Estate racket. Granted, it comes with a lot of work, but what it needs the most is a lot of connections because the permitting process is next to impossible. They did it. And all required communications, water, electric, roads and more. To make a long story short - Father happily retired..., pardon, rested. Two sons, however, found themselves in a pickle. The farm is now smaller. Agriculture prices are lower than ever, while costs are thru the roof. Then Georgia passes the law making seasonal workers ineligible for welfare assistance during off-season months. There is nothing to do on a farm for all those people during winter. Down South they don't pay nothing for nothing. And like this - pfui - all their employees disappear.

We Laughed.

From the rear-view mirror I saw a real-life Cullen Bohannon. I mean, the guy really looked a lot like a protagonist of AMC's series *Hell on Wheels*. Bit more rounded. Minus the stupid hair.

Mr. Bohannon type - they don't fret, they don't flinch, they just keep at it.

No matter what.

Through a 'job broker' (I'm not kidding - A JOB BROKER) they hired a Guatemalan Crew, who costed less even considering a temporary housing that Mr-Bohannon-look-alike built for them. Guatemalans worked so hard and fast that Southern Gentlemen had to give them some paid days off. Tobacco didn't grow fast enough for those guys.

No complaints.
Always in good mood. Always happy.

Farming has been an 'idee fixe' of mine for some time, so I had some questions. He was happy to oblige and I learned a great deal about rotation of cotton with soy or corn. Some intricacies of tomato irrigation and fertilizing weren't so new to me, but a certain kind of Yellow Pine - that was a discovery. Apparently, there is a sort of Pine tree used for lumber, which matures to production in only 7 to 10 years. So what you do is - cut some trees on your property (read: forest), replant clearing with new Pine trees and continue doing it every 2 years in equal parts over next 10 years.

Forest Farming FTW! Fucking brilliant! How come nobody mentioned this when I was looking at that farm near Poconos a few years back? That place wasn't really a 'farm' - most of it was just land with forest on it. Very costly to turn into arable fields, but perfect for Cullen Bohannon pine shticks. Guess people Up North don't think like that.

(Papa B spits)

The Man in Blue Suit from Georgia doesn't work on the farm anymore. The profit just isn't there to support two households, so he left it for older brother to take care of Family Land. He now sells insurance - that's what Philadelphia trip was all about - insurance for big industrial green-houses, which evidently can be done in a morning meeting and lunch at unfriendly to Southern stomach eatery.

As I listened to his slow and calm voice, I started to get a sensation in my neck and back of the head. It's really weird, and wonderful, and happens very rarely when I talk to like-minded people. People who share my values in life. It's like waves or something I can neither describe clearly, nor understand fully. Funny thing - I can feel this woovy bliss long after the person I caught the vibe from leaves. Hours, sometimes days after...

By the time we got to the Airport I was tripping.

We both removed sunglasses and shook hands. I think I saw a hint of surprise in his stare... and smiled. Real-life-Cullen-Bohannon took his time collecting his phone, charger, back-pack and neatly folded jacket, wished me well and slowly walked toward Delta entrance. Not 'slow', like lazy, fat or sick - 'slow', like steadily putting one firm step in front of another. Wide strut. Broad shoulders caring a hard-chinned head. I watched him like I watch a rare animal from far away land. May be exotic, possibly near extinct, definitely not from these parts. I seldom look at my passengers after they disembark Beloye Taksi - a person has to be really interesting for me to gawk...

Georgian was almost at the door to the Airport when he slowly turned, looked at my car from front to back and then at me. Dead in the eye.

THIS never happened before.

His name is Marshall, but even if it wasn't, I would still call him that.

Chapter 2

Rate Race

Uber App – the front end that we see – runs on extraordinary sophisticated Algorithm, based on rating system. I don't pretend to understand how it does it, don't know what the code looks like, but I have a firm grasp of what algorithm intends to do and explain the best policies to use it properly.

Anybody can get a ride to drive at some point in time, if he waits long enough. The ride with far away pick-up, low rated rider who doesn't tip but leaves a mess and pay-off too small to matter – a gypsy cab. Professional full time Uber driver can get a job (a ride) almost anywhere at any time, a nice long ride with high-rated passenger and a tip with 5-star rating at the end. Luck is just a part of it – gypsy cab driver got lucky. A Pro will put himself in front of Algorithm, making it easy for computer program to find him, by being at the right place at the right time and having a high rating.

Five-Star Rating

There are several rating schemes going on at the same time. The focus seems to be on a Star Rating – an average of last 500 rated trips on a scale of 1 to 5 Stars, both riders and drivers give each other. Although no official guidelines have been published by Uber, the word is that 4.3 will boot you off the system. Indeed, I have never seen 4.2 Stars rated rider. No doubt, the 4.3 threshold is arbitrary and probably fluctuates depending on local situation. I guess that more miserable places will have lower average Star Rating, while pleasant ones will have higher.

All Star Rating does is weeding out crazy drivers and filthy assholes, and discouraging all kinds of bad behavior in a car… with swift and irreversible judgement. The health and longevity of ride-sharing as a service depends on it and its value cannot be overstated. Riders continuously judge performance of the driver and smoothness of the ride, evaluate cleanness of the car and courteous attitude. 5 Star is normal – it's what expected. In Uber, half of the riders don't leave any rating at all, while drivers must rate all trips, making rider's Star Rating more accurate at this time. (In Lyft – all ratings are optional.) My Star Rating has been stuck between 4.91 and 4.95 for a long time, because of few 1-Star reviews (probably due to some political discussions I had).

While the main function of 5-Star Rating is to make sure that maniacs don't drive and psychos don't ride, it is also used to differentiate quality of service (both given and received) and to make assumptions about the future. Algorithm expects that 4.9 driver will remain on top of his game (that's how he got to 4.9 in a first place), continue to provide excellent service and drive responsibly. Uber's computer is set up to pair high rated drivers with high rated riders, all other things being equal. But all other things are not equal, far from it, making Star Rating not that important – for making money, that is. Now, this last statement is not a reason to stop washing windows and vacuum floor mats. Just don't worry so much about what some condescending prick clicked on his ridiculously overpriced Chinese phone. Rather focus on following these rules:

Rule # 1   Safety First

Rule # 2   Courtesy is the Best Policy

Following key Rules #1 and #2 will inevitably result in many 5-Star ratings, generate tips and make life healthier and more fulfilling. Unfortunately high Star Ratings don't automatically translate to higher profits, they just make these profits easier to achieve.

Internal Ratings

Professional Uber Driver needs to focus on two other numbers in the 'Ratings' tab of the app – Acceptance and Cancellation Rate. I call them 'Internal Ratings', because riders can't see them – only Uber can. These ratings are the key to making more money faster, reducing downtime and getting longer trips (hopefully with some high-rated passengers).

The driver has a choice of accepting or declining the ride (press 'No Thanks'), when a call comes over Uber App. The highest Acceptance Rate of 100% means that driver has taken all jobs offered over past 7 days. What happened 8 days ago doesn't matter anymore – it is gone from calculations. If a driver did 50 trips over past 7 days and didn't accept just 1 request, then his Acceptance Rate will fall to 98% and will stay as such for next 7 days (unless he declines more trips... lazy bugger).

Uber Algorithm wants us to take all jobs no matter what, because it is good for the whole system. If a driver refuses the request the call goes to next driver down a list, and if the next driver refuses too then it will go further to other neighborhood drivers and then again until somebody takes it or the rider looses patience. Customers don't want to wait, they just want to "press the button and have a car appear". Algorithm is set up to do it quickly and efficiently, and will favor drivers who hustle hard and don't clog up the works. Accepting all jobs is simply a good business – the customer is happy that a car is on the way, the Algo humming along crunching out directions, the driver is moving making "money-honey"… life as it ought to be.

And why would you not accept a call? What, is the pick-up too far away? Well, first of all - they ain't gonna come to you. You are the Transporter, but first you need to pick up who you are transporting. Besides, what alternatives are there – to sit by the side of the road, waiting? I would rather take a job and go make some money. Hey, it could be a 2-hour long highway trip (the most profitable one).

What, you don't want to take 'Pool' request at 11pm on Saturday night? Well, I have done 'Pools' so long – they were the biggest fare that day. Besides, what if you refused 2 'Pools' in a row late on Saturday (because MAH SUPA UBA only takes 'X'-class riders during premium hours), and an 'X' passenger you finally got… pukes all over back seat… Bad karma, I guess. Should have taken that 'Pool'. (It actually happened to me – just like that).

So I made a rule to treat all people equally respectfully and work responsibly by taking every single job that comes along, and Uber Algo loves me for it.

Cancellation Rate is even more important to driver's earnings and success of ride-sharing as a service. Let me be blunt – to 'Cancel' is the worst sin a driver can commit for the system and will be punished severely by Algorithm. Don't cancel, look for your rider, wait for him, do everything you can to complete your job. Call and text the rider thru App to coordinate pick-up.

Drive around the block to see if he is there. Do whatever you can to make the pick-up, except don't get out from the car – it's against Rule #1: Safety First.

Exceptions:

- Cancel only when you tried everything else and there is no rider to be had.

- Cancel only when you don't feel safe!

I will come back to these special cases, but first I want to address a misguided notion going around You-Tube that 'Cancelling' is the fastest way to make money. It goes something like this: *Arrive close enough for your pick-up, but park in a way that they can't see you right away. Don't answer any of their calls or texts and don't reach out to them. Wait until App flags 'Cancel with receiving a cancellation fee' option. When asked for a reason, check 'Rider no-show' and be on your way. Easiest 3 bucks.* Right?

Wrong! As your Cancellation Rate grows, your Internal Ratings plunge and Uber Algo starts giving preference to other, more dependable, drivers. And why shouldn't it, since you treat your customers so rudely and make ride-sharing unreliable. Try to put yourself in rider's seat. A person just wasted time waiting for a car that never "appeared", got charged 5 bucks (or more) for nothing and now has to call another car and wait again. How do you expect a customer like this to be satisfied with service? That person will hate all Uber drivers – a bunch of conniving snakes, and probably deem this Uber thingy as irresponsible and untrustworthy. Not a type of conditions for a healthy growing business. Not as advertised.

It happens often enough for riders to mention it to me again and again, as it is one of the worst consumer experiences imaginable. Think about it: remember when you got stood up by some plumber, or when cable guy showed up 3 hours late, or when you had to wait 2 weeks for electricity to get restored after winter storm? How did it make you feel? Well, don't do it to others, don't 'Cancel' and Uber Algo will love you for it, give you more work and better rides.

Then there is another wrong-footed view that cancelling difficult riders is very important for protecting driver's Star Rating. Let me set the scene: *A driver cannot find the rider right away or address is wrong. Driver calls. The rider is agitated or drunk and is not in cooperative mood. Driver kind of gets a feeling that they will be pissed at him regardless and will give him a low Star Rating at the end of the trip anyway. So driver 'Cancels', because cancelled rider cannot leave a rating.* Well, what can I say, this type of driver is either stupid or lazy or both.

First of all, as I explained, Star Rating is not THAT important. A couple of 2-3 Star reviews will not make a huge difference for total ratings and will not impede money-making ability very much.

Secondly, yes, Uber navigation can serve inaccurate location or wrong address. Sometimes you have to be a little bit like a detective, think with your head and use one tool App doesn't have – your eyes. Look, it's not a great mystery: there is a person somewhere by the side of the road, desperately in need of going someplace. Call them and talk to them like to a friend who asked you for a ride. Don't explain and don't complain, instead be constructive and business-like.

Their rotten mood may not be directed towards you at all. Maybe he had a rotten day at work or she had a fight with boyfriend and now this Uber nonsense – stupid driver is lost or parked 2 blocks away in a rain. You are not clairvoyant, you don't know what is going on or what is going to happen. But, who knows, maybe a miserable person like this gets into a fresh-smelling car, with pleasant music playing, and during a smooth ride their mood improves. As rider relaxes in a back seat of Beloye Taksi, he (or she) may appreciate this change of pace, even become friendly and reward you with a tip and 5-Star. Why not? It happened to me many times, just like that, although it is not my intention to be a mobile shrink.

Don't forget – late or not, pleasant or not – you get paid for your services on the spot. Shouldn't it be enough of a motivator – 'Cancel' and you get nothing; don't 'Cancel' and you get riches, stars and gratitude of your fellow man.

The choice should be clear (I think):

Rule # 3   Take All Trips and Do Not Cancel

While I cannot think of any reason not to accept a trip, there are a couple of important provisos for 'Do Not Cancel' part. According to Rule #1 – it is driver's Safety First. If something looks wrong or smells fishy – just run and 'Cancel'.

Ambush

I had this situation inside big apartment complex one late night. After waiting an obligatory 2 minutes, I called the rider to confirm that I am in a right place. The guy on a phone sounded weird and sort of menacing. I didn't like it right away, turned the car facing an exit from the parking lot, put it in gear and started carefully watching my surroundings.

Few more minutes passed when I saw them come out of the apartments, and it looked very wrong. There were 6 or 7 of them, too many for a 4 passenger Uber 'X'. I thought: "Maybe some traveling and some just saying good bye or going to their own cars", but they kind of faned out and were approaching my car from the back and both sides. This is very unusual behavior – normally people go as a group or in a column, plus I saw them carrying small objects that didn't look right either. I don't know if those were stones or water bottles, but two of them had long sticks that definitely looked more like baseball bats than umbrellas.

I started driving slowly to maintain some distance between them and Beloye Taksi, thinking that maybe it's all nothing, they will wave or yell "Uber don't go" and later we will all laugh at chicken-shit driver (me). Instead these fuckers started to run silently and when I saw one of them throw that stone (or water bottle) at me – I just floored it. After driving for a few minutes and making several turns to make sure nobody followed me either on foot or in a car, I parked up all covered in sweat and 'Cancelled'. All according to Rule #1 – Safety First - my safety first and foremost.

Hey, if you are paranoid it doesn't mean they are not out to get you. Be careful out there!

Rule #1 also covers the rider and the car. Especially with regard to passengers – their safety and wellbeing is the driver's responsibility. Sometimes people just don't know what's good for them and can put a driver in a situation where no safe service can be provided. Like the day when...

Baby on Board

A woman with a tiny newborn baby got in the car. No car seat. I have taken preschool kids without booster seat to day-care before. If they can sit still, buckle up and don't stand up during the ride – I'm OK with it. A little two month old baby needs a rear-facing child seat. Period. And I told that woman as such.

She started to plead with me that she is buckled up and she will hold baby tight, but I wouldn't have any of it.

I said: "Lady, God forbid we get into an accident, you will be fine buckled-up and all that, but your baby goes into windshield and I go to jail. <u>Do you understand this?</u>"

Clearly she did, as she bolted out of the car, straight into the house she came from. I tried to reach out, called and texted, but she never came back and did not answer. So, I 'Cancel'.

Drunkards are a constant concern, as it is impossible to predict how an intoxicated person will behave. Most are fine, can hold their liquor and will not make a mess in a car. I have this guide – if they can walk to the car on their own and get in without assistance, they can ride.

Sunday Drunk

One Sunday morning I got a request from a guy so drunk, he could not walk. Hell, he could not even stand up without holding on to a tree or a parked car.

I saw him fall twice, but it didn't seem to bother him at all. Poor guy was all covered in dirt and visibly shaking.

Honestly, had it been late that Sunday, I would take a chance – put him on plastic, give him a Red Bag to hold and hope for the best (I've done it before). But in the morning… all I was thinking: "Bastard is gonna make a mess in my light interior'ed car (sic) and I will spend better part of Sunday cleaning. IF I can get it all washed and dried today… Big IF…"

So I explained to him that I am not his Uber and that he should wait sometime and sober up before calling a car, gave him a bottle of water with some paper towels, 'Cancelled' and left.

These situations are quite rare, but do happen and cause Cancellation Rate to rise above 0%. If a driver 'Cancels' 1 ride out of 50, his Cancelation Rate will go up to 2% and will stay as such for 7 days. On day 8 that cancelled ride will drop off the calculation and Cancellation Rate will go back to 0%, unless more rides get 'Cancelled' by the driver. (Not to get confused with riders cancelling their requests – it's different and doesn't apply here)

<u>What sets top rated drivers apart from everybody else are these Internal Ratings.</u>

As you, dear reader, can get from my tales, Internal Ratings can and should be kept INSANELY high – Acceptance at 100%; Cancellation at 0% - for as long as possible, but it will not last forever. Sooner or later something will preclude you from accepting a request. Your phone will hang or you will be helping someone with luggage or something… and you miss a request. Sooner or later you are going to 'Cancel' for whatever reason and your Internal Ratings will take a hit. Importantly, Uber Algo understands this too and will not penalize driver harshly if Internal Ratings slip by 5-10% (Acceptance of no less than 90%; Cancellation of no more than 10%). So, now your ratings are not INSANELY high, you are no longer the top rated driver, but you are still HIGH up there and Algo is still your friend.

Chapter 3

The Girl in a Mink Coat

The Algo

Uber runs on extraordinary sophisticated and complex software package I call Algorithm or "Algo" for short. To be a successful Uber driver, one needs to understand what it does and act accordingly. There is no live person watching drivers and riders – Algo does it; there is no bookkeeper to calculate fees and charges – Algo does it; there is very little customer support involved (used to be none at all) – Algo does most of the work.

All Factors of Algo operations are readily available for Uber drivers to see, but they are not explained clearly anywhere. I had to figure all this out myself by observing both the driver's and rider's apps at the same time and making detailed records. I've taken subtle clues hidden in Uber's online manual and app itself, and also other notions offered on interwebs, and checked them against a wealth of data provided in the driver's app. Uber supplies drivers with a mountain of data, covering most aspects of operation, compensation and quality control – absolutely FREE. I organized and analyzed these facts and figures to infer how this app actually works – what makes an Algorithm tick. If I know how this machine is programmed, I can do exactly what it wants for maximum efficiency by putting myself in front of it and on the very best spot.

Obviously, my next ride is absolutely random – "it's like a box of chocolates, you never know what you are going to get" – except I can skew the odds tremendously in my favor and make more money faster and easier over time. Neither I, nor software know the future, but Algo functions on making assumptions about it and driver has to do the same. This diminishes the role of Luck in success as a Professional Uber Driver and turns this 'gig' into a money-making Business. Chasing Luck (in general) is a fruitless pursuit, because Luck favors prepared. One has to put himself in front of Luck in all endeavors of life by doing the right thing All The Time – in other words, following a Rule-based system.

This chapter explains how to prepare to get Lucky, with one important proviso – I actually don't know how this software is written and have no idea what computer language they use. I completely reverse-engineered this thing for the end used (the driver), not for computer programmer. Also, I am pretty sure that Uber people would neither confirm nor deny my inferences, but to be on a safe side I took care to avoid all contact with them, so there is no conflict of interest or intellectual property concerns involved. Terminology is my own. I came up with most definitions and hope they are easy to grasp.

The Cell

The key to understanding Algo is Uber's Cell structure. When prospective client enters the app they see a Cell of about 7 cars in close proximity. The Cell could be of any shape (it doesn't have to be a circle or a square), so one has to use a little bit of visual imagination to draw an invisible boundary in a mind's eye. This Cell applies only to location of a 'virtual' rider. Any cars further out are not shown. Any cars arriving into Cell's area with passengers are not shown either, but may be used by Algo to compete for next order. Any cars going 'Online' near rider's location will cause the farthest car to drop off the Cell, making the Cell region smaller and changing its shape. There could be nearly infinite amount of Cells overlapping each other, because each prospective client will create his/hers own cell by simply entering rider's app.

Most of the time a Cell will have 7 cars in it. In the City, sometimes they are only 2-3 blocks wide – with cars parked across the street literally sitting on top of each other in app's map. Maximum size of a Cell is limited to 25-30 minutes of travel time from the center (where rider is). I often find myself late at night out in countryside dealing with one of those huge Cells, 40 minutes to an hour across with several towns in-between. They used to be major pain, considering possible 20-30 minutes ride to pick-up for a $3.50 fare, but now Uber pays for long pick-ups, so it's not so bad. Lyft does not pay for long pick-ups at this time. I expect this to change in the future.

When a customer enters an order into app, all 7 cars in the Cell get rated based on multiple Factors and take position in a queue. The top placed car in a queue gets order request first and if he refuses then order goes to a second car in a queue and so on down the list until somebody picks up the request. If everyone takes a pass, then request goes around again from top to bottom of queue until customer loses patience and quits (which is very bad for business – very, very bad). In reality this scenario rarely happens, because the top rated driver in a queue will take the job, and that's it. He will accept request right away, because this is what top rated driver does – he follows Rule #3 - Take All Trips.

Factor 1 – INSANE Internal Rating

The most important and heaviest weighted Factor in calculating queue position is Internal Rating. Keeping Acceptance Rate at 100% and Cancellation Rate at 0% almost always guarantees top placement in a queue, all other factors being equal.

I checked it many different ways, recorded and compared results. On a busy Saturday night none of it matters anyway, because there is plenty of work to go around. For the rest of the week, INSANE Rating makes all the difference between an Uber who gets the job without waiting and go make money and the other six drivers who will continue to sit in a shade airing out their socks. See for yourself: drive at Insane Rating or as close as possible for 4 weeks. (Note: I am pretty sure that Algo uses some kind of longer measure, like a 4 weeks moving average or median number or 3 best out of 4... at least I would.) Record and analyze your results. Then do the opposite – don't take Pool, don't take pick-ups more than 10 minutes away, 'Cancel' at will and so on. Methinks that by the end of week 2 of this brodacio, Rule #3 will become clear as day. Nothing hits harder that the heaviest thing in the World – the Dollar. You will feel this hit in your wallet – I guarantee it.

Do the right thing, treat everybody with respect, follow Rule #3 (Take All Trips and Do Not Cancel) and Algo will reward your dedication and responsibility by offering you work first, before everybody else.

Factor 2 - Distance

It is only reasonable to assume that the car closest to a rider gets the job. Unfortunately, in reality, it doesn't work like that all the time, because of other Factors involved. Indeed, I often get requests far away from visible to me Cell, only to find a couple of other cars sitting near my pick-up. Other Factors were so high in comparison to nearby drivers that they overpowered proximity consideration and placed me on a top of the queue.

Lady and the Fools

One day, as I was moving through Main Line, request comes from 20 minutes away in Conshohocken. I'm like: "Hmm, interesting, no cars in Conchy. I got to get back there when I drop off this passenger". As I'm standing on a light at Matsonford Bridge, I put rider's app on – lo and behold, there are 5 cars surrounding my pick-up spot. That's pretty cool. Woman is waiting beside the road looking at a phone, sees me coming, goes directly for rear passenger side door. Knows what she is doing, not a noob. Doesn't slam the door, but gives me scorched earth look and remarks that she waited ridiculously long.

"Why didn't this stupid app give me the car I see sitting across the road?"

I say: "Lady, you are a very high rated client, they had to send for me. Only the best for our most valued customers, glad to be of service" and blah-blah-blah.

That definitely took the wind out of her sails, though she tried to muster another attempt at misinformed logic.

"Well, what about those other drivers?"

I say: "Lady, those guys can't get a job even if one falls on their lap. They are deadbeat lazy fools. You, being a top rated rider, get matched up with highest rated driver around these parts. I hope tomorrow you get someone even better than me, but today you can relax in quiet, safety and comfort of Beloye Taksi, partake in sugar-free candy and quench your thirst with finest natural spring water of Pennsylvania. Enjoy!"

No, I didn't actually say any of that shit, but I do provide high quality individually wrapped candy and mints, as well as tiny bottles of spring water, all according to Rule #2.

I also vividly remember a $10 cash tip, 5-Star and written compliment – a full sweep. Nice.

So, obviously, this is an unusual story. Normally, distance from a rider to nearby cars matters quite a bit, especially in suburbs and countryside, where I drive most of the time.

Algo will go for nearest driver, all other Factors being equal. It is important to understand that Factor 2 (Distance) is absolutely random – we really don't know where prospective riders are, we can only guess. It's a lot like fishing – we can use experience and knowledge to locate good spot, get there early, use right bait… and still come home empty-handed. Fish may have been there, but they didn't bite and just swam by. That's life.

Fortunately, there are ways to increase chances of a car being within short distance from many possible clients (as well as to fish with two poles, but that's for later). Think about it this way: people live all over the place, but they eventually move to places of "Mass Activity" – office buildings and industrial complexes, shopping centers and malls, entertainment areas with bars and restaurants, etc. You stand a better chance of finding a rider where riders congregate, so go there. Don't drive aimlessly around, but move towards a location where prospective clients should be, based on common sense. Check rider's app to see what your Cell looks like – make sure it covers one or more areas of mass activity. That's where the fishes are.

On the other hand, it is important not to get overzealous and do something so obvious everybody gets it, like going to a stadium at the end of a game or concert. At a place like this, there will be 100's (even 1000's) of cars leaving parking lot, on top of army of Ubers, Lyfts and Taxi-cabs, all sitting in one tremendous traffic jam, sometimes for hours. There is no advantage to be gained from Factor 2 – we all are within same distance from prospective clients, but it probably doesn't matter anyway because there is usually enough work for everybody. Of course, the allure of these places of "Extreme" Mass Activity is in getting a rider going an hour away back into suburbs, but I never caught one. All I ever got were people going to houses or bars 20 blocks away… in traffic… if I was lucky to find them in a crowd… Complete waste of time.

Look, what happens here is "People are Not Stupid". In fact, they are very smart. They Uber to a friend's house or a restaurant during the day. They pre-game there and wait for late friends to arrive. Then they walk or Uber to a stadium – all very safe and cost effective and fun – the whole process takes several hours. After the game, they migrate in reverse order, but all at once. Prices in app surge by 2-3 times (even more), because of great demand created by huge number of overlapping Cells. Algo sees all these Cells created by every rider's app that goes 'On'. Algo freaks out, anticipating an avalanche of orders, and jimmy up the prices into a stratosphere. But people are not stupid, they know this will happen and plan accordingly, getting me to fight traffic for the next 2 or 3 hours. Yea, sure, I get triple fare... a whole 10 bucks. Meanwhile, they wait it out on friend's roof garden or at a café, prices collapse and only then hundreds of very drunk and very tired people Uber-Pool home, puking all over back seat. No sir, thank you, but I'll pass.

Instead of following the herd, I look for an edge – a small advantage over other drivers. Sometimes you have to think critically, look few steps ahead and be a little bit of a contrarian. When I can identify a place of "Extreme" Mass Activity – I go away from it as far as possible, and catch a streak of non-stop jobs for hours.

Superballer

When a local team was playing semifinal game in town, I didn't go into city, but instead went 20 miles away, deep into Bucks County. Although app never registered any surge prices, there was a great activity. Jobs were coming non-stop, all evening long. I haven't even arrived yet, but a new order was already coming for acceptance. I took them all. I had one party disembark and another one immediately gets in, in the same location, several times that night. From restaurant to bar, from bar – home, from another home in the same development to a restaurant and back to bar. Up and down Bucks and Montgomery Counties - the game was on TV everywhere. Even cops watched it in their cruiser, because there was nothing for them to do – there were scarcely any cars on a road. I looked at a rider's app several times – holly bogolly, it's like I'm the only car from Southampton to New Hope. The map was nearly empty.

So, seriously, I probably wasn't the only Uber in suburbs. There must have been others, but they were busy like I was and were not visible on the map. That Cell must have been huge. There was no way to estimate its boundary or shape. Still, I stick to a couple of big roads (Street Rd and County Line) – roads with shopping centers, restaurants and bars - to keep my distance within reach of many drunk and happy football fans.

I was making $50/hour for several hours with no surge pricing (straight up), while everyone else was sitting in the City… in gridlock… making minimum wage amidst public celebration on the streets.

You can put yourself smartly in front of Luck, and it will hit you – head on!

To keep yourself within "Lucky" distance from many possible clients do this:

-   Look at rider's app. (Just don't do it while driving.)

-   Zoom out enough to see your entire Cell.

-   Make sure there are areas of mass activity inside your Cell.

-   If there are large empty areas on your map (lightly populated countryside) or if it includes parks, lakes or forests – you are at disadvantage for Distance Factor. You are too far away. I will return to this.

-   Don't sit inside residential development, large business complex or deep inside mall parking lot. Algo will take it into account, thinking that it will take you too long just to get to a main road, and will give you a lower queue position.

-   Recognize places where Distance Factor doesn't matter or not being used in calculation of queue order, like airports or train stations where everybody parked together. I don't pick up in Airport.

Factor 3 – Vector

Listen: Uber is a <u>ride-sharing</u> app.
In order to get jobs, you have to be <u>riding</u>!

The direction and speed consideration (Vector) are deeply ingrained in functionality of Algo and (I think) one of the main Factors in calculating driver's position in a queue. **If two cars are within same distance to prospective client (with all other Factors being equal), the car that is moving will get a job before the one that stands still.** The logic behind Factor 3 is iron-clad: the car that is moving on a road will get to a client faster than one that has to get out of parking lot, make left on green, and so on. Vector Factor has a limitation: if a car is moving at speed of over 60mph, Algo will assume that this car is on a highway and drop it to the bottom of the queue. You are useless to Algo on interstate – there are no riders there. Even if you do get a request off the highway, it may be a major headache.

Crack in a Matrix

One time, late at night, I was coming home from faraway lands and got a request while balling 75mph on the Turnpike. I don't know if I put the app 'Online' automatically or just forgot to turn it 'off', but it definitely wasn't my intention to drive anybody there and then. I just wanted to get home, still, Rule #3 and all that...

so I took it. Sure enough it was 20 miles to next exit and then another 15-20 minutes to get back to them.

Once I realized what was going on, I reached out to the rider thru app – called them to rectify the situation. I was like: "Listen, if you want to wait 40 minutes – I will come and get you, but this is some kind of a mistake. There must be cars closer to you. Maybe you want to cancel me out, order again and get a car near you?" They did.

There are cracks in a matrix and sometimes computers do weird things, but normally Algo likes to see you moving at speeds of 20 to 40 miles per hour and uses your Vector of movement (Factor 3) in assumptions about your Distance to prospective client (Factor 2). Distance and Vector are interconnected. Together, they are the second biggest consideration in calculation of driver's position in a queue of a Cell.

A 'Normal Road' is a perfect place to put Factor 3 (Vector) to driver's advantage. A Normal Road has 1-2 lines in each direction, separate turn lines, traffic lights, no center divider and speed limit of 25-45 mph. A Normal Road goes thru towns. It has shopping centers and office buildings, hotels and apartment complexes, gas stations and restaurants, etc. It usually has a number. Drive down a road like this and BOOM – a request comes in. Rule #3, followed by Rule #4, always using Rules #1 and #2... may all your rides be smooth.

A driver that is sitting somewhere beside the road with windows down feeding flies has no Vector and will have to compete with other drivers for a position in the queue, based on other Factors. This may not be so easy – there are a lot of high rated drivers out there doing the right thing. To make most money in an efficient way, a driver has to put as many Factors to his advantage as possible.

"Keeping up the Vector" – moving at average speed on a Normal Road – has a certain leeway. Algo doesn't actually watch you every second, it sort of keeps an eye on you periodically. I can't say for sure how often car's Vector gets measured, but I think it's about every 1-3 minutes. When a string of these measurements makes no progress, Algo assumes that the car is parked and drops its position in a queue somewhat. On the other hand, if Vector measurements show some movement (even sporadic – in fits and starts), Algo will think that you are in traffic or stopped at a light, but it will know that you are on a road actively looking for next fare, and will treat you accordingly.

Naturally, there is a way to game Factor 3 a little bit - Keeping your Vector Up, while not driving endlessly in circles, wasting gas. Do this:

- Drive down Normal Road for about 5-10 minutes.

- Look for a spot to safely park on a side of the road. Make sure not to break traffic laws. Wait 5 minutes.

- Drive again, then stop when possible. Algo will think you are moving in traffic and will not penalize your queue position at all. Make sure not to stand more than 5-10 minutes – Algo is watching!

Many Normal Roads don't have parking lane. Hell, most countryside roads don't even have a shoulder – just a monster ditch beside the road. No problem – just go to next intersection and look for a pharmacy, McDonalds or any kind of store or shopping center with parking. Get on that parking lot and stop as close to the road as possible, facing same direction you traveled before. It may be harder to do during the day, because you may have to park across several parking spaces – perpendicular to markings on pavement, but parallel to the road. If you manage to get close to that road, Algo will think you are still on it, merely sitting in traffic. Make sure not to be on a sidewalk and not to obstruct other vehicles.

The following two Factors are of lesser importance, they are also much harder to gain and don't change very much over time.

Factor 4 - Star Rating

I already covered it before.

Be a nice guy, drive responsibly, keep your car clean and treat everybody with respect – Star Rating will follow. After 500 5-Stars your rating will change very slowly and in small increments, so you will know exactly where you stand.

Factor 5 - Heat Index

When a driver who doesn't drive consistently goes 'Online' - he (or she) may not have a single job for an hour or two. A driver like this is 'Cold' to Algo. As time goes by, driver gets 'Warmer' – Algo sees a person 'Online' for an hour or so and decides that he (or she) means business, starts to take that driver more seriously and raises a position in a queue somewhat. To escalate Heat Index to 'Hot' reading will take a whole lot more than that – it will take time, determination and dedication – good old-fashioned hard work.

Algo knows a great deal about its drivers. Since most drivers who quit do so in 3 months or less – Algo has a minimum tenure requirement. Up until three months of driving, Algo will not consider a driver as a 'serious' partner and will dump him (or her) in queue ranking in favor of older, more experienced drivers.

There is more. Three months is just a stepping stone. The real threshold is 2 years, pretty similar to any other 'normal' job.

Alongside with acknowledging tenure, Algo also analyzes recent work patterns. Full time driver spends no less than 25 hours 'Online' per week with a break of no more than 3 consecutive days. (They probably use some kind of 4 weeks moving average, or median number, or 3 out of 4… at least I would.) Full time driver will do minimum 50 trips per week (often much more) and quickly achieve other milestones – 1000 trips, 500 5-Stars ratings, etc. – each increasing their Heat Index a little bit.

Imagine a guy – driving for about a year, couple of thousand trips, almost a thousand 5-Stars, 4.92 rating, working over 25 hours per week – he is already 'Warm' to Algo. He puts the app 'Online' and starts boiling even faster. Within 10 minutes he is 'Hot'. BOOM – request comes in. Indeed, I have to be careful where I put my app 'on', it may not be a job I want. And, of course, there are people out there who are even 'Hotter' to Algo than I am. There is nothing fancy in getting 'Hot' – just show up for work every day and don't take long vacations.

Proper Factor Alignment

A Driver who

- Has INSANE Internal Rating;

- Moving at normal speed on Normal Road;

- Thru areas of Mass Activity;

- Highly 5-Star Rated;

- And Hot as Fuck

Will get a highest quality job first,
in front of all nearby drivers, no matter what.

I would like to posit that
80% of meaningful work out there is
handled by top 20% rated drivers
(and some Vilfredo Pareto dude enthusiastically agrees)
Think about it deeply.

The following is my guess. I really don't have any way to test this, but I think that these are the weightings that go into queue position calculations:

Factor 1 - 50%

Factors 2 and 3 – 15% each

Factors 4 and 5 – 10% each.

I could be off but not by much, because these Factors are not some digital files – they are based on Taxi-cab experiences of 'old and their many shortcomings Uber attempts to overcome.

Taxi Girl

Shortly after coming to America, I got a job driving for a Taxi-cab company, covering West and South Philadelphia. After only couple of weeks they gave me a car with a radio, which was a big deal. (Not all cars had radio back then and nobody I knew had a cell phone.) I was excited to finally be able to go straight to a client, instead of driving aimlessly around downtown looking for pick-up.

Radio turned out to be bunk. First of all, it didn't work very well, but mainly it was just pointless – all jobs went to a select group of drivers. It didn't matter if I was closer, they didn't even acknowledge my call. Those Taxi Girls – the dispatchers – were almost mythical creatures. They knew whole town like a back of the hand and could give detailed directions at a moment's notice. They knew where best jobs were, they knew where people are going, they knew where most of drivers are. They knew it all down pat, but wouldn't tell me.

I was lost and hopeless, until one day I saw two of them walk out of the office after shift change. Taxi Girls wore mink – top to bottom – with Louis Vuitton bag in tow and Mercedes on a parking space. I saw a couple of guys walk across the yard to them. I saw a couple of envelopes change hands. I knew what I saw, took some money out from my sock and went across the yard.

"You are that rooky Russian kid they gave a radio to?" – older Taxi Girl croaked.

"So my radio isn't broken – she really sounds like that," I thought and just smiled.

There was nothing to say – money was doing all the talking.

"We gonna see 'bout keeping you busy 'ut there. Don't be a stranger, come and see us next week, tell some stories".

Her breath smelled of cigarettes, her coat smelled too – that ridiculous mink, too warm for the weather. But I knew why she wore it.

If you, dear reader, think that I am making too much hubbub about all these Factors, Cell, queue and so on – reflect upon a Taxi Girl for a second and her task of dispatching the best, most experienced drivers to closest riders. Uber Algo does that and more, completely devoid of shitty office politics and personal favoritism, always fair and objective, entirely lacking mood swings and intestinal gas.

Uber Algo is THAT Taxi Girl, minus a fucking mink coat.

UBER TALE

Lolita

I drive around colleges a lot. There is always business, especially Wednesday and Thursday night. I really cannot understand this propensity of American youth to party in the middle of the week, just when one needs to be alert and lucid for work and study. Why not party on a weekend? Isn't it what it's for?

On Wednesday night around 2am, this half-naked girl gets on a front seat, all sobbing and crying. Nymphetka is definitely drunk and with a slight whiff of bud, although it's so faint she could have just stood around people who sparked up. The ride is short, plus I've been hustling over speed limit to move things along, as work comes in without any breaks. A thought of offering her a tissue crosses my mind, but tissue box is in a glove-compartment so I would have to reach over her legs and that is kinda awkward.

May be I should offer her water?

Nah, she may throw up.

I decided to shut up and just mind my own driving business. We almost arrived anyway... When sobbing intensified I had to glance at her quickly.

O god, please… Not on a dashboard… Can she hold another minute or two?

Guess she thought my look was a disapproval of her and Lolita had a sudden urge to apologize. I assured her that I am nothing to worry about, doesn't bother me at all and that everything is OK. We arrived.

Convinced that I don't understand, Nympha was overcome with urge to explain.

"He broke my heart."

I smiled with relief – she won't puke.

"It's gonna be OK."

Why do I always say these idiotic things? It's like the most lifeless, 'I don't give a shit' kind of response.

"NO, it will NEVER be ok. 40 years from now, it still will not be ok. How he could DO it? What do I do NOW?"

"Don't think BIG thoughts at night, wait until the morning light."

"WHAT?"

My words get gargled sometimes. I wanted her to understand. I repeated, slower now.

She was on a front seat, leaning towards me. Eyes glowing like brilliant sapphires. Lips flowing like a river of honey. Neck vein thrusting like a bloody abyss.

I wouldn't dare to even glance any lower. "There are limits to self-control", I thought, as I felt driver's door armrest ream into my spine. Face burning in a blast of desert heat. Arms numb like they are not even there.

"Darling, you don't want to do THIS", I rasped.

"WHAT?"

She suddenly slumped. Spared from succubus gleam, I was able to breathe again.

"THIS. You are right. Even 40 years from now, it will still hurt. You are going to remember this heartache for the rest of your life, but it will get better with time. Except THIS. THIS will feel really shitty... forever. Go to bed."

"Oh, you sound just like my daddy."

The devil was on a rise again, infused with some Freudian bullshit no doubt, but I already snapped back.

"My dear, you need to go sleep. Don't talk to anyone. Don't do anything. Straight to bed, you hear. You have to get up in a few hours. There are things to do tomorrow, or rather today. Right? Any tests tomorrow? Go to bed. NOW."

I was going nonstop, like it was my only saving grace, seeing how she is coming back with every word until the little teenage schoolgirl reappeared. Cold and tired. A moment later Nymphetka was gone.

I put the app 'Offline' and went home.

God damn it, WHY, in the name of Zeus's butt-hole, I couldn't be a sleazeball sugar daddy for ones in my life when such a great opportunity presented itself. I could have done anything to that girl. Shit like this just doesn't happen to guys like me. What's wrong with me?

I was tossing and turning until early morning light and when I finally fell into slumber Lolita was back. I can't control what I dream, so that's that.

Chapter 4

Papa B's Evil Game Plan

Philadelphia area and surrounding suburbs and countryside are not unique at all. In fact, Philly is right around statistical average on almost every economic and social metric of the entire United States. We got a little bit of everything around here – ghettos and extravagant mansions, industry and nightlife, farms and skyscrapers, and peoples of all colors and origins. If you live in other places, take my experience as a guide. Look for similarities to your local area – you should find many, but probably not all. For the rest of it, dear reader, follow my logic and do your own thinking.

Uber's Philadelphia territory extends for over 50 miles around the city (over 2000 square miles). It is not uncommon for me to visit every corner of it within a week and sometimes on a single day. I go wherever road takes me, but my intention is to hit highest quality and most profitable areas as much as possible. I approach this ride-sharing 'gig' as a Business, and I live off of it. As such, the objective is to figure out how to make most money in a shortest period of time, with the least wear and tear on a car, as little stress as possible, and with smallest amount of risk.

'Most money' is actually the easiest to understand. Uber pays more per mile driven than for minute spent on a trip. At the present time, they pay us here about 90 cents per mile (was a little less, now a little more – it fluctuates), and 15 cents per minute. New Jersey pays less, Delaware pays more – it's a bit different everywhere, but surprisingly makes you about the same amount of money. Small differences aside, 'Time' portion of fare adds up to about minimum wage. That is all they are making sitting in traffic jam – 5-10 dollars per hour. On the other hand, if you are driving on a highway at over 60mph, you are making that 5-10 dollars every 5 minutes. It just makes more sense to seek out trips for longer distances, because driver makes more money faster and highway rides are easiest on a car. The Holy Grail – a 2 hour trip to New York, 100 miles there and deadhead back, will easily yield $20/hour pay, if not more. I take Normal Roads back (the one without tolls) and find plenty of work on a way home, making long trip even more profitable. Unfortunately, long trips are few and far between, but not to worry – I've got the next best thing – 15-30 minute rides over 10-30 mile stretches. A skillful and experienced driver can string few of these together and (with a bit of Luck) make $20-30/hour on average, but <u>not every hour and not all hours</u>.

Zone Strategy

To understand strategy involved I need to explain my Zone Strategy - a way to identify locality and quickly ascertain action needed for maximum profitability. There are 5 distinctly different types of territories or 'Zones' within Philadelphia area, each offering its own benefits and challenges. <u>There is work in every Zone</u>. There is no strict boundary between these Zones, they often overlap each other or go in some striped fashion to the extent that I decided not to make a color-shaded map, but to keep a general concept in my mind's eye. Other places around the country may lack one or more of these Zones – I will offer examples. I don't believe there will be variations, but you will be the judge of that where you live.

RED Zone

City of Philadelphia (only about 150 sq. miles out of nearly 3000 available for driving) is divided according to Rose of the Winds. Most of the City (Center, South, West, North and part of NorthEast along I-95), also Chester and portions of Norristown, Pottstown, Coatesville are a RED Zone, characterized by color of most of it in an app. Pretty much any time, day or night, and especially during rush-hours these areas will be … RED, meaning the prices are surging or there is a boost in effect. The prices are high for a reason: everybody is sitting in a traffic jam.

Indeed, congestion on the streets of Philadelphia is horrendous – a short 5-10 minutes trip takes 30 minutes in traffic during the day. At night, Center City turns from business downtown into party and tourist destination, while parts of West and North Philly become very inhospitable and dangerous places to be. Drivers pull back from the ghetto and go downtown, where they promptly get stuck in traffic created by incredible density of population in the City. Algo sees all that, gets all worked up and doubles the prices. Higher prices in this case are not really extra higher income, but a feeble attempt by a computer program to compensate for lost revenues (Taxi-girl-minus-mink-coat is trying…). Generally, people of RED Zone don't travel far – they live in a city where everything is close by, with many rides going for only few blocks. In other words: the rides in the City are too short in distance to make a difference even with elevated prices – you'll be lucky to make $10/hour.

Some people say: "It's OK. I go make $10/hour for few hours near home." That's fine. Just make sure you understand the limitations, like disastrous road conditions in the City that will take its toll on your car. A City driver needs tire balancing and wheel alignment more often than usual because off all the potholes, and caverns, and ridges, and mounds they make in place of potholes. I'm talking trenches so big, one of them swallowed an entire wheel of a city-bus last winter. The thing got stuck in there and had to be jacked up. Crumbling roads not enough? How about constructions?

Regardless of terrific overpopulation, they continue to build. Skyscrapers go up, colleges expanding, old houses being gutted and rebuilt, whole blocks getting facelifts - real estate speculation going full blast.

I just have one question: "How are all these 'new' people going to get there? All the streets are gridlocked already. What? Are the flying in?" Constructions, city repair and maintenance, high vehicle count and extreme density of population all contribute to (uncharacteristically) high for America pollution levels. City stinks.

I guess you can see where I am going with this:

Rule #5   I Do Not pick up in RED Zone

It has few important exceptions that I will explain further in the book, but first, I want to clarify that I will take people to absolutely everywhere in RED Zone, and so should you. Nobody should be refused the ride based on a destination of where they are going – this is not how this Uber thingy works. So, I will go anywhere, but if I see that my ride lands some place I don't want to work – I just flip 'Stop New Requests' in app and that's it. Otherwise, I might find myself stuck between ghetto and City Hall, watching my time circling down the drain.

Yellow Zone

Most of NorthEast Phila, Lower Bucks County, some of Norristown and Pottstown areas (and sporadically everywhere) are Yellow Zones. Surge prices here are not a permanent fixture and they usually don't go red (2-3x), but stay kind of yellow (1.1-1.5x). Yellow Zone is still a city with pretty high density of population, but with much less traffic. Quality of life is better here, streets are wider and cleaner, roads are generally in better condition. There are numerous plazas and office buildings... without bars on windows.

Population of these areas is "Working Poor" – they are OK, have jobs, cars, many own their homes, but they don't have any money left after paying the bills. There is plenty of work in Yellow Zone, although still shorter trips, they are faster to complete and will pay better than RED Zone on average. People who live in Yellow Zone (working class) tip exceedingly well, especially on a weekend. I live in Yellow Zone.

GREEN Zone

"GREEN" for money, cabbage, mulla mucho grande. The best place to make money is the first band of suburbs, extending for about 20 miles beyond City boundary. There are a lot of people there very close together, but many of them live in newer, bigger, single houses – so standard of living is visibly higher. GREEN Zones will still have apartments here and there, but some of them are actually luxury condominiums.

There is a lot of activity in the GREEN – shopping centers and malls, gyms, spas – all the good stuff for affluent clientele. Locals have means, they have disposable income and they spread it around 24 hours per day.

Philadelphia GREEN Zone has another added benefit, some localities in America may lack. See, when business and industry moved out of Philly due to burdensome regulations, high taxes and crumbling infrastructure, they moved to... GREEN Zones surrounding the City. Nearly half the people I drive on any workday evening are regular, everyday folks merely going home from work. They go to their rowhouses and tenements from jobs at pharmaceutical factories and industrial complexes, hotels and hospitals, giant office buildings and private mansions. They go from GREEN Zone back to Yellow and RED. A lot of them go in a 'Pool', which is kinda crapshoot in suburbs. Density of population is not enough to produce additional riders all the time, so I basically end up driving people for less money. There is no reason to cry over spilled milk, Rule #3 dictates taking all trips (even in suburbs), besides these rides are usually longer anyway – so it works out all right.

GREEN Zones are characterized by noticeable amount of rich people. You will see spacious neighborhoods with McMansions and extravagant gardens, upscale shops and gourmet restaurants and every type of watering hole imaginable. These are the clients to look forward to - they use Uber regularly, tip consistently, very polite and clean – a pleasure to work with. They go to airports. They go out on a weekend. Their children Uber <u>all the time</u>. They are so rich – they pretty much don't care how much it is. My wife asked me: "If they are so rich, why don't they have their own personal driver?" I reply: "Why, honey, they just send for me."

While inhabitants of North and West RED Zones of Philadelphia city rarely travel across I-76/Schuylkill River, people of North and West GREEN Zones travel across pretty often. They go from Ambler to see relatives in Downingtown, or go from Collegeville to party with friends in Media, dropping 30-50 bucks, simply because it's convenient. They take Uber to Bronx for a $150 fare in a middle of the night, so not to worry about parking in NYC. They be like that guy who got me to go to nearest liquor store in the depths of winter, he didn't want to wait for his car to warm up and preferred to have me wait by curbside so he doesn't have to walk in the cold… and leaves a $20 tip. GREEN is the place to be.

Blue Zone

Beyond GREEN Zone, and sometimes intermixed with it, lies countryside with Blue skies everywhere you look. There are no tall buildings here, no apartments, but a lot of subdivisions with single houses, old farm-like properties and pretentious new developments. There are lakes and forests in Blue Zone – it's quiet and the air is crisp.

I often reflect how, only about 100 years ago, "Old Money" of Main Line landscape looked exactly like many Blue Zones do in early 21 Century. In time, most of Blue Bucks and Montgomery Counties will become "Old" as well, will turn a shade of GREEN, in concert with constantly shifting RED and Yellow. Memento mori.

Blue Zone will have some mass activity centered around major intersections, but there is no density of population to support anything like what you find in GREEN or Yellow, don't even hope. There is not a lot of work here, but at the same time there are not a lot of drivers either. Cells in Blue can be half hour wide even during a day, and especially at night. If you wait awhile, or better, move toward nearest town or nearby GREEN Zone (to Keep your Vector Up), there will be a job to make that wait worthwhile. Hell, I picked up people from places where it takes 10 minutes just to get to a main road, and then I drive for 10 or 20 miles. Blue Zone rides are usually long, locals know that and (more importantly) are able to afford it. No problem.

White Zone

White Zone lies beyond GREEN and Blue. If you look at territory far removed from the City on Google map, you will notice that there are vast swaths of emptiness – clear blotches, with only few roads and small towns that are not shaded. The map is almost White.

These are farmlands, mountains and forests, where there is no density of population and mass activity is scarce. I was surprised to find residential developments and retirement communities there. There are people, but they are widely dispersed. Locals are astonishingly polite and well mannered.

Farmer John

They be like that Farmer John, who gets in with dirty farmer boots covered in poop-n-soot. We get there, he gets out, turns around, reaches inside a cab, grabs onto floor mat. I'm like: "Brah, no stealin' a fucking floor mats. Na' mean?" Scared a poor farmer half to death – nice man wanted to shake off the dirt he brought into my light interior'ed car – he was cleaning after himself.

I hope I get to drive him again, I hope to drive people like that every day of my life. After living in United States for almost 30 years, I finally found America!

The Cells in White Zone are gigantic and often don't even have full 7 cars in it. Not a lot of drivers are needed here, which gives me a great edge with my city-level ratings. White Zone drivers have a problem – they can't get Hot. It's impossible for them to get 100+ rides per week average of a city driver. My average is actually lower – I do 50 to 100 rides per week, due to limited time spent in a City, but even that is enough to bump me to the top of the queue.

Added benefit is my INSANE Internal Rating. It takes a lot of discipline to keep taking requests and constantly going for pick-ups 30 minutes away. (This is when I looked at my sleep-deprived, black-eye-baggy face in a vanity mirror: "Dude, this shit is crazy! It's INSANE.") Eventually people get frustrated or decide that they don't have enough time, refuse the request and… tank their Internal Ratings, giving me an upper hand. I don't get bogged down by long pick-ups, I follow the rules – Rule #3.

If I find myself late at night, somewhere in Lancaster County (Amish country) - streaking down a windy country road, high beams blazing, Modern Talking blaring - I am pretty sure that my Beloye Taksi (White Cab) is reigning supreme over the White.

Once Zone is identified, your actions should be clear:

- If you are in a GREEN Zone – good,
  Keep your Vector Up, be ready to get busy.

- If you are in Yellow, Blue or White – wait, or start moving towards nearest GREEN Zone.

- If you are in A RED Zone – get out (Rule #5), by using Relocation Technique.

Relocation

Say a driver finds himself in West Philly late at night, somewhere south of Fairmont Park and a bit west from U-Penn (an ivy-league college) – in a middle of the Hood. RED Zone no doubt. Driver puts his app 'Offline', travels north-west across Route 1/City Line Ave. and BOOM – Ardmore – America the Beautiful, GREEN as Benjamins. Driver puts his app 'Online' and CRAP! Request comes in from back south, from the OTHER side of Route 1 – Back to the Hood (Rule #3).

"Just when I thought I was out, they pulled me back in"… naturally, it's a 'Pool'…lol.

This type of situation can be avoided by monitoring rider's app, while moving away from RED Zone. Look for cars behind you to see when you get far enough for them to disappear from your Cell. Remember that this Cell is a figment of your imagination – it's originated from your location and applies only to a hypothetical rider located where you are. In reality, we don't know how many prospective clients are out there, each creating his-and-hers own unique Cell, but we can create a moving picture in the mind's eye and have a realistic estimate like this:

- When moving away from RED Zone, look for other Ubers in RED Zone to completely disappear from rider's app.

- As soon as it happens, take a note of 2-3 cars farthest out in a direction you are traveling (I assume you going to GREEN Zone, right?), and remember their location.

- Chances are that once you get there, RED Zone is so far behind that no common Cell will include it – you are free to harvest GREEN.

If only all Relocations were so easy. Most of the City of Philadelphia is so to say "landlocked-shut"- you can't get out of it in short period of time and good GREEN pastures are far away. People migrate towards City all the time, day and night, for multitude of reasons. It's as if the City attracts them like a magnet – if I get too close, I will eventually find myself in Temple University... in the middle of the ghetto... one of America's best inside one of America's worst... only in America, but I digress.

Finding myself somewhere in a City is a good thing – that means I successfully picked up a ride faraway in suburbs and drove them here, making at-least $20/hour. Now I'm facing 'dead-head' – an old trucker's term, meaning "driving with empty trailer and not getting paid". To minimize amount of time needed to get out of RED Zone (Rule #5), I use Relocation Technique based on Anchor Points (fancy name, eh, I spent a whole day making it up).

Anchor Points

As I traveled through GREEN Zone, I took notice of places near exits off major highways. I was looking for WAWA (local convenient store), or 24-hour pharmacy or a McDonalds – a store with clean and publicly available restrooms. I also wanted a gas station nearby, so once I get off a highway I can go get gas, a cup of coffee, wash my face and be ready for work in short period of time. I programmed these locations as Favorites into a separate GPS unit (TomTom), so I don't have to look for address or shuffle the map on a phone. I got places like these all over GREEN Zone – they are Anchor Points for Relocation.

Once I drop off a passenger in RED Zone, I can quickly set directions for Anchor Point closest to nearest highway. I don't mind if it's extra 10 miles, a couple more dollars of gas is not a problem. I simply want the fastest route to get out, so not to waste time. I want to get deep into GREEN Zone as soon as possible, and get a nice $20 ride that will pay for that extra gas and more, much more. If I can safely park up in RED Zone, I may check several of these Anchor Points and traffic conditions along the way. Sometimes going even further may be fastest after all.

Example:

- I'm in Center City, towards Delaware River.

- Closest Anchor Point is Sunoco on Rt30 in Ardmore. Going thru downtown, across Schuylkill and up Route 30 (Lancaster Ave.) is 25 minutes and usually more in city traffic. Plus, the wheels are coming off my wagon, quite literary. This Anchor Point is closest to RED Zone.

- I can get on 676 out of town and go north on 76 (which is usually packed), take a left onto 476, exit at Villanova and go 4 minutes to Anchor Point in Wayne, pure-emerald GREEN. 30 miles, 35 minutes at night, but at least 45 during day. Wayne is a good place to be at night and on weekends, because of colleges all around and lots of bars and restaurants in the vicinity.

- Let's say Wayne is no good, because traffic is at stand still on 76. Fine, I can get on 95 South, go past the Airport, make right on 476 and go to Anchor Point in green-eye-GREEN Media. This is shorter (20 miles) Relocate, which also takes 30-45 minutes depending on traffic. I especially favor Media Relocate early in a day, because it opens me up to an immense expanse of Blue to the West of West Chester. I don't seek out Blue Zone in the evening, because if it pulls me into White late at night – I will be so far away from home, I may not see my wife until the next day. During a weekday, Blue Zone is a prized destination for the driver from the other side of town – there is no traffic there at all, rides are long, competition is lame – with any Luck, I may not get back into Philadelphia until late night.

By quickly plugging different Anchor Points into TomTom GPS I can decide in less than a minute what place deep inside GREEN Zone is the fastest to get to. I try to keep these Relocates to less than 1 hour, preferably no more than 20-30 minutes. Originally, I found Relocate to be a major disappointment. This deadhead really cuts into hourly earnings. On a hectic day (when everyone wants to go downtown), my average hourly pay can be sliced in half. Meaning: although I was making $30/hour while 'Online', I go home with $150 after 10 hour day. BTW, $15/hour is an average reported for ride-sharing drivers. I make more. You can too. But not in RED Zone.

After a few months of adhering to my Rule-based system, I learned to enjoy these breaks in the daily grind. I get a chance to call my wife (hands-free): "Hi, honey. I'm Relocating. I can talk…" I can eat a sandwich while leisurely cruising on a highway or listen to an audio book. I don't need a boss-man permission to put my windows down or to turn the heat up. I'm on a break. Fuck off.

Relocate Anchor Points starting west of the City, going clockwise: Media, Newtown Square, West Chester, near Downingtown, Malvern, Wayne, Ardmore. Hop on north of King of Prussia – outside of Phoenixville, Skippack, Hatfield, Ambler, Warminster. Few of the distant ones in Doylestown, Quakertown, etc. I got places in New Jersey. I keep finding new, better ones all the time – if it saves me travel time, if it puts me into better location, if I can shave minutes off my pit stop – into the Favorites it goes.

Each of my Anchor Points is also an area of Mass Activity – I expect to get a job right off the parking lot, once my break is completed. My Anchor Points are located on or near Normal Roads, so if I don't receive a request within 5-10 minutes, I can start moving up Normal road thru GREEN Zone, having all Factors in my favor, doing the right thing in the right place. I don't want to provide exact addresses of my Anchor Points in this space – what's good for me may not be someone else's preference. But you, dear reader, can use this logic and pick your own favorite spots. The key point here is this:

Anchor Points must be prepared in advance and saved for easy retrieval:

- So you don't have to scroll through Google maps, while sitting in a middle of the Hood at night.

- So you don't waste your time, stuck in traffic.

- So you don't get lost on suburban backroads.

This last point is actually a very useful added benefit of using Anchor Points. Say, you drop off a passenger in a big and curvy suburban neighborhood, a dozen turns deep into it. There is no point sitting there – you don't have a Vector and your Distance Factor is abysmal. You are too far away from anything and Taxi-girl-minus-mink-coat doesn't want to deal with you. What do you do? Start putzing around with your map app, figuring out turns by twisting fingers?

No. You punch directions to a nearest Anchor Point, and go. Navigation will get you out of any boondocks and onto a Normal Road. So, immediately, all Factors are in your favor: you are already moving and Keeping your Vector Up, your Distance is changing and your Heat Index is high. Do not put your app 'Offline'. You are moving towards an Anchor Point in an area of Mass Activity. There is work there. Meanwhile, as you travel thru various lands, you may get a pick-up request for somebody going to that area of Mass Activity anyway. I mean, all those people I drive home, first had to get from home to all those places where I pick them up. No?

Exception to Rule #5

If during the day on weekday I drive a 'Pool' into RED or Yellow Zone (even into ghetto), then I don't turn the app 'off', but continue to take additional riders with expectation that they will eventually throw me out away from the city or land near a major highway.

Indeed, on more than one occasion I had 'Pools' that originated in north GREEN Zone, took me thru north RED Zone of the City, touched downtown and then jumped from South Philly to Darby and out on Main Line – about 2 hour trek and possibly the biggest fare of the day. Make sure to monitor driver's app to see if your path leads out of the City. Once route of the trip begins to bend into circle – pull the plug and exit thru GREEN door.

Intersection Trick

A situation can be created where a car has a favorable Distance Factor to multiple areas of Mass Activity at the same time. Think about it: I don't know where the next job is coming from, but by increasing amount of places it is <u>likely</u> to come from, I can decrease waiting time.

What you are looking for is an intersection of two very busy Normal Roads, like Street Rd and Bustleton Ave, on a border of Philly Yellow and East GREENish-Blue. These kinds of roads are full of shopping centers, business complexes, hotels and apartments. They will have very few single houses and no forest around for miles.

Intersection Trick requires advance planning. You need to find a place to stop (even better – a series of stops), less than quarter mile before that intersection. This stop will be about 5 minutes long (to Keep your Vector Up). Use shoulder or parking lane where available, but don't break traffic laws. Don't use bus stops and *No Stopping Anytime* lines and don't block traffic. This shtick can be performed on hydrants, driveways and small near-road parking lots, but only for a couple of minutes.

I often put my hazard flashers on, during performance of these Tricks, in order to alert other drivers on the road that I am about to do something out of ordinary. If a cop comes by, simply act normally, keep your hands where they can see them, and say that you had to safely pull over to work out your phone. Resolved.

Meanwhile, you check rider's app to size up the situation, while Algo still thinks that the car is moving towards an intersection. Algo will take your Vector into account and plot a course to next rider, regardless of where it is – left, right or straight – all favorable for Distance Factor. It's like shooting Gatling gun in comparison to a revolver.

In the Cell

I have made several assumptions:

- Highest 5-Factor rated driver in a Cell will get a new order first, no matter what.

- I am not a highest rated driver in the World.

- There are a lot of people like me, with similar ratings.

Therefore, when observing locations with other cars in the vicinity, I don't want to stay with a group of other drivers, because chances are there is somebody out there with even higher rating than mine. I usually have choices of direction, especially after Relocation deep into GREEN, so I prefer to pick a heading where competition is light. Working smarter <u>and</u> harder.

In Uber's rider app – <u>moving</u> is the only way to see other cars, beyond 7 visible for a Cell centered where driver is. Sometimes, on a slow day, it seems that all I'm doing is running away from swarms of other Ubers. There are a lot of very clever people, hustling hard out there.

In Lyft's rider app – map can be moved to reveal hidden cars, but things will change by the time I get there (because Lyft's Cells are generally bigger).

Airport

I don't pick up in Airport. It's a waste of time. Once I drop off a passenger, I get on 95 south, make right on 476 north and either exit into Media or continue to Wayne, GREEN as can be.

I'll be done with my pit stop and complete a ride or two, while the rest of those guys sit in their cars under open Airport skies, farting into seat cushions.

New Jersey

I work in New Jersey a lot. There are few small, isolated RED Zones – Camden, Trenton, Newark and some parts closer to NYC. Everything else is a giant mix of GREEN and Blue, with patches of Yellow. You can drive a whole day without a single Relocate – no deadhead at all! Taxi-girl-minus-mink-coat knows it… and pays less per mile and per minute than in Philly area. Take home pay ends up being about the same, plus roads are pretty good, people are nice and scenery is just magnificent (especially in Watchung).

Papa B's Garbage Can

Princeton area is one of my all-time favorite places to drive – billiard-velvet GREEN. I've met some of the most unusual characters on rides from Princeton University. Like a (no more than) 15 year old kid, who didn't talk, didn't take a candy, didn't look out the window, but kept scribbling something in his notebook. Dual major – theoretical physics and applied mathematics… or was it the other way around? Baby Einstein, you 'no.

Or like that woman, visiting to watch her youngest son compete in ivy-league swimming competition. Kid was winning, she was proud and on a way to Princeton Hyatt, no less. She told me about her three kids, two of whom already graduated Princeton before. They were from Hong Kong.

I was seeking out certain financial types, so I can talk shop. Wall Street crowd is plentiful in GREEN-back circles of Princeton Train Station, as well as at BlackRock, Dow-Jones and other financial monstrosities around there. What I found, as a result of my interviews, was alarmingly disturbing.

One ride stood out. I had a professor of political studies and another guy of similar stature, but in socioeconomics. We had a lively discussion about present state of affairs. As a matter of discourse, I offered a variant perception of some recent developments. Fellow 'scientists' were thoroughly impressed by my parley prowess and remarked that "even cabbies are intellectuals in Princeton."

Buildings on campuses have names – names of wealthy donors, who shelled out all or largest part of cost and operations of these buildings. I will never make anything close to the amount of money it takes to name a building. But I do have an Impossible Dream that someday there will be a place on every campus where all kinds of people can peacefully debate and exchange views, openly and in plain language, without constrains of political correctness, which suppresses critical thought and handicaps pursuit of truth.

In a center of such places I edict a structure to be erected - Papa B Memorial Garbage Can, topped with stoned' ashtray, conjoined bong and grinder, strapped with a water fountain and stuffed with a solar-powered wasteless trash compactor… One can dream, right? I'm sure my professor compadres would enthusiastically agree.

City of Brotherly Love

*(Warning – imagine my face while reading this like
I'm talking to you in a pub – screaming, red eye bulging,
vein popping, spit flying... but totally making sense.)*

Big part of City of Philadelphia is the ghetto.
Boom! Immediately people think I am a racist when I say
it, because they equate "ghetto" with "nigger",
misinterpreting cause and effect.

Ghetto got all kinds of people – black, white,
hispanic, etc., but that's not the point. Most peopleS
inside of Philly ghetto are remnants of sizable and
relatively financially secure working class. See, up until
about 50 years ago, Philadelphia had a strong industrial
base, many factories and a very active port. At some
point they called it "textile capital of United States". Then
it all went away and took their jobs with it. Now we have
a significant portion of City population who did not have
meaningful employment in three generations.

Family values, morality and integrity go out the window when you don't have steady paycheck, regular family dinner around the table in cozy home and nice vacation with wife and kids to look forward to. The degenerate lifestyle entrenches over many decades and becomes the norm – they simply cannot see it any other way and distrust people trying to show how.

It's not like "all the niggas are dumb". Not at all. Most of the ones' I see are actually pretty smart, street smart, wise smart. They try to 'break out' as best as they can, and many succeed. That's normal. There is a certain sliver of population, who does not want to leave the ghetto, but came there intentionally to stay and be completely invisible to authorities – you can live your whole life in the ghetto, totally on cash basis, with no ID, address or taxes. Also, there are people who, accidentally or through substance abuse, slid to the lowest level of society. They "crossed 110th street" in a wrong direction, so to say. They came here to die – mortality in the Hood is on a third-world country level. Whenever I drive across North or West Philly, all I can think of is: "These people need help. A lot of it."

"What kind of help?"- you ask.

Well, how about taking a big military medical ship from the Gulf or China Sea, or whatever faraway place across the globe. Put that hospital ship into old Navy Yard and get busy. Look, 90% of these people are sick. All kinds of sick – from heart disease, diabetes and arthritis to drug addiction, depression and psychosis. They are really, really sick!

More? How about taking hundreds of millions of dollars of aid we send to countries, nobody in the ghetto can point out on a map, and dumping all this ALREADY free shit around Hunting Park and Wissahickon? These people can really use it – clothes, supplies, building materials and more. They really need this shit because they are hopelessly poor, they have no money and no prospects of making money to buy this shit.

What? Drugs? Listen –
EVERYBODY KNOWS WHERE DRUG DEALERS ARE!

(I warned you: we are in a bar, probably drunk by now.)

Ghetto is in terrible condition. Potholes big enough to swallow entire tire, intermixed with mounds made in place of previous crevices. Dilapidated, burned out buildings blend in with crumbling sidewalks, littered with garbage that haven't been swept since the time Reagan was in Office.

Speaking of the Oval Office. Recently, POTUS ordered some 60 Tomahawk rockets to be fired somewhere on the other side of the World, but only like 30 went to target. The rest were lost. I know where they went – to Philly ghetto! Some parts of it legit look bombed out. No joke.

Funny, how the same President opined about some third-world countries being shitholes. I would like to take the gentleman, hand-in-mother-fucking-hand... to the Hood, so he can observe the horror and breathe in the stench of shithole right here at home – practically in the center of the Cradle of American Liberty.

Sometimes by choice, but mostly by neglect, ghetto dwellers became ignorant, useless and hopeless. They don't possess no useful skills and don't seek no knowledge (sic), because it is not needed. There is no meaningful employment to be had and no hope of it coming back to the City. There is work outside the City, but they can't get there. Remember: poor people – no money, no car, no suit. Of course, there is a widely developed transportation system, in the City that is. In Bucks County, buses stop going after 6pm with only couple of routes operational once an hour till midnight. I saw them. Those buses are a joke – they had like 3 people in them. Hell, I drove more people in 'Pool' today and every previous day of the week.

It may come as a surprise (at least it was to me), but fully half of the riders I drive on weekday evenings are normal everyday folks of all colors simply going home from work. I pick them up from all kinds of occupations – higher paid manual jobs, cleaner and better positions, even new and promising careers. I pick them up in the suburbs and countryside and take them home – back to the ghetto and surrounding parts. They had no way to get to that kind of work before Uber. What are you going to do: Hop on a train or a bus... and then hike like 3 miles thru the woods and highways? Uber and other ride-sharing services are changing my beloved City of Brotherly Love, right as I'm writing these lines.

By the Book

A quarter past 7 on Friday, I picked up Rocco again, for a third or fourth time, near pharmaceutical plant outside Lansdale. Just like before, he was going home to Chew Ave in a 'Pool', but this time he was unusually cheerful. He announced that this may be the last time he takes Uber - because he was putting some money aside since he got this job about half a year ago, and now had enough to buy a used car.

"So, you be driving here all by your lonesome", I quipped.

"For realz. Even better – Ama gona round, find me-self mo' money paying ja' or get a second ja', cus I ain't need to sit in UBA for 2 hours no more."

"That's pretty smart in my book."

My heart warmed with joy.

MAH UBA has taken a small but instrumental role in lifting one soul out of poverty. Helping my fellow men to help themselves. I will continue to do my part. How about you?

Chapter 5

Time Tactics

Your experience driving for Uber or any ride-sharing company (the kind of jobs, the type of riders and the amount of money) will largely depend on the time of day you choose to spend on the road. The allure of being your own boss comes with heavy responsibility – you have to send yourself to work during hours you may want to rest... or play.

The Party line goes like this: "You can work your own hours, when it is convenient to you." To which I reply: "Yea, sure, but it better be night and weekend hours or you are never going to make any serious money otherwise." I want to be clear – there is work everywhere and all the time, but not in the same quality and quantity.

Let me take a day apart for you and offer my observations. Starting around 5am, we get a 'morning rush'. A lot of rides are needed in GREEN and Yellow Zones for several hours. City is the place to be in the morning, as crime rate drops to almost zero and work is available throughout. Morning people are typically late for work and they get further frustrated sitting in traffic. Surprisingly, there will be longer rides (30 minutes plus), but these people will be going to industrial areas, or truck drivers going to their parked rigs, or construction workers going to boondocks. Once you get there, you are stuck, there are no rides to be had – you are too early and too far away.

Around 10-11am, business goes into 'lunch lull' and stays sporadic until 2-3ish. My wife asked me: "Can't you work normal hours, like everyone else?" To which I reply: "Why, honey, all people who take Uber are at work – they don't need no rides while working. People who don't work can't afford no Uber, you 'no." Except this one thing that makes day driving profitable and fun – Airport trips. This is what I do: I go out after the 'morning rush' subsides. Straight to North GREEN Zone (anchor point Ambler), because it's the farthest from the Airport. North GREEN has everything I need – industrial and office areas to the west, pharma and colleges to the north, dozens of hotels to the east and people of affluence and means throughout – the kind of people who fly a lot. Basically, sooner or later, I am going to the Airport for 30-50 dollars (or more with surge). I don't pick up in the Airport.

From the Airport – I have options. Returning to North GREEN Zone is out of question – it's the longest Relocate, but I can go left to Media and work a giant GREEN/Blue Zone west of the City, far away from traffic, RED and smog. Alternatively, I can jump on 95 and go home to sit out 'evening traffic jam' that paralyzes all main roads from around 4pm to (sometimes) past 7pm. I rest, and eat, and see my family instead of sitting in gridlock, making minimum wage.

Chapter 5

Whenever I work on a weekday, I make sure to leave house (in Yellow Zone) anytime between 6 and 7pm and go straight for nearest GREEN Zone. Things will start hopping around 8pm and it will get more interesting from that point on. Most drivers will go home after 10pm, tired and irritated after fighting traffic for 14 hours – just when the going gets good and all the roads are empty. Along with usual crowd of people going home from work, we get the most fun, highest tipping, 100% repeat clientele – partygoers. Wherever Uber reached capacity (meaning: there is a car 15 minutes away, day or night), DUI offenses go down by 60-80%. There is no reason to drink and drive anymore – they can get an Uber for the price of one drink – and I'll be there to scoop them up. I am pretty much guaranteed to be making $20-30/hour in GREEN Zone between 10pm and 2am, unless it's a 'hump' day. Typically, Wednesday or Thursday night will be slow, but a couple of long rides should make up for that (that's what high ratings are for). I also noticed that there are absolutely dead days some time before or between the holidays, but I could never guess right in advance. The best approach is to show up for work every day and let the chips fall where they may.

Late night note: just as I found it to be smart not to drive during 'evening traffic jam', I think it's wise to avoid 'last call for alcohol' crowd around 2-3am. These are the meanest drunks, followed by total weirdos after 3-4am. If I find myself close to home after midnight– I just pull the plug and call it a day.

The best days to drive are Friday night, Saturday, Sunday and most holidays. I have made more money on Saturday, than on Monday, Tuesday and Wednesday... combined!

The question whether to 'push it' or not is very personal. I know that I have pretty high endurance – I can work several 12-hour days in a row without getting fatigued or sleepy, fully lucid and alert, with cheerful disposition towards my passengers. Then the weekend comes and I am going to milk it for all its worth, sometimes 'pushing' myself into 14-15 hours Saturday, unless I get very tired. I will not jeopardize my safety and lives of other people for 20 bucks.

I rest on Monday, as all limo drivers, wedding photographers and celebrity hairdressers do.

Don't forget about your own wellbeing – exercise regularly every day... by thoroughly cleaning your car inside and out. I call it Gypsy Zumba – you bend, you stretch, you move around, without needlessly wasting time on pointless exertion, aka gym. When people ask me how I manage to keep my light interior'ed car so spotless, I say that I don't clean so many times per day – I clean all day, every day.

<u>If you have time to lean – you have time to clean.</u>

I usually do my scrubbing, wiping and disinfecting after Relocate – a convenient opportunity to get out of the car anyway, as I was driving for hours, floor mats are covered with wet grass, water bottles are gone and one of the candy cups needs refilling. I think that it's easier and less time consuming to keep and maintain car in pristine condition, rather than let everything go to shit and then spend hours on all fours - rubbing, scraping and shampooing. Cleaning is not optional or occasional thing to do, it has to be done per Rule #2 - Courtesy is the Best Policy. You want your customers to be in 'comfort' – it's a simple Courtesy to provide clean environment, basic amenities and pleasant vibe. I plan my time for cleaning as a part of work day, and out of respect for my office.

As you, dear reader, can see from these observations, it may be uneconomical to go out driving for only few hours. A driver needs a <u>long</u> working day of 9-12 hours to cover several time periods when jobs are plentiful and rides are long, and also Relocates, Intersection Tricks, pit-stops and occasional honey-do's. It is also advantageous to come out open-ended. Meaning: there is no certain time by which you need to be somewhere. This way you can let the road take you anywhere by selecting the strategy best suited for Zone/time combination, and continue working until you run out of clients, become tired or arrive home.

Chapter 6

Money

Let's face it: driving for Uber or any other ride-sharing service is a menial, low skilled, albeit very high tech, labor. As such, it CANNOT pay a lot. An average hourly rate in USA has been around $25-26/hour for years. A Professional full time Uber driver, with tenure and high ratings, should be able to pull it regularly. Rooky - occasionally. Lazy fool – never. An average pay for an average driver will land somewhere in $10-20 per hour range and depends a lot on how you count your chickens.

To know exactly how much you are making, what it costs you and to find ways to improve is divine. Not knowing your true state of affairs will lead to miscalculations, disappointment and... you may lose money. So, grab a pencil and a notebook – we gonna get some numbers outa this jawn.

The most important question is how to count hours worked. Typical job start paying the moment a person is clocked in, once they are there, leaving out time needed to get to work. I had a good one on one with my boss... in a vanity mirror. "Pst, look here asshole. You be paying me the moment I step out the door. You be treating your employee with respect and dignity, you hear?" Of course, he agreed. (It's not madness to speak to oneself, as long as it doesn't talk back.)

My situation is not unique, but probably will not apply to everybody. I live in Yellow Zone, so on many occasions I drove literally from my back-yard parking – there is plenty of work around here. However, after careful consideration and armed with some numbers, I decided that potential profits are higher on average if I don't work right away, but travel 30-40 minutes, deep into nearest GREEN Zone. Because of that, I always start my day with this deficit – a time wasted for initial Relocation.

I think about it as a matter of Fear and Greed.

I Fear this loss of time for Relocation – I'm not making money, how am I going to pay my bills, what am I going to tell my wife;

when I should be Greedy – I'm going into GREEN, to drive rich men and flowery women, on a highway, and get tips.

I am Greedy – I want to get out now, and make ten bucks, to pay for gas, right fucking now;

when I should be Fearful – I'm going to get maybe 4 short rides in a next hour, and the fifth will pull me deep into North Philly, from which it takes over an hour to get out, after they take ALL the candy.

1.   Record the time from when you get out the door of your house to the moment you are back at that door. Realize, that from now on your hourly pay will be lower than widely quoted numbers, but it will be true and real. This is your Total Hours.

2.   Record amount of Miles driven from door to door. From the app, record number of Trips given, hours spent driving passengers or actively looking for a ride (Online Hours) and how much you made that day (Money).

3.   Following financial analysis works best if it is based on a long continuous workday of 9-12 hours. If I drive in a morning, then come back home to rest and go out later in the evening again, then I make separate row for each in my notebook, and call it a 'Split Day'. In the past, I have also split days on purpose to compare different combinations of Zone and time of the day. I encourage you, dear reader, to perform your own tests to confirm my findings and have a way to adjust when things will change (as they always do).

4.   Divide Money by Total Hours. This is your True Hourly Pay, including deadhead, breaks, cleaning and errands you decided to run while at it. There are ways to increase your own Hourly Pay by better strategic planning, strict time management and pissing a little bit faster.

5.   Divide Money by Online Hours. This is how much you are making, while your app is 'on'. It is also a much higher number than your True Hourly Pay, sometimes 2 or 3 times larger. Remember the highest recent Online Hourly Pay – this is the number you tell your relatives at a next poolside barbeque. Really? Sure it is, and I can prove it – aren't statistics great? (tips hat)

6.   Divide Money by Miles. If you make $1/mile or more – you are golden – keep doing what you're doing, you don't need any advice from me. If you make less than 50 cents per mile – you are in trouble – either drive a little less between the jobs and use more Intersection Tricks, or try a totally different Zone/ time combination. My average is between 60 and 80 cents per mile and I can go for 200-300 miles without breaking sweat.

7.   Subtract Online Hours from Total Hours. This is your deadhead and downtime. The ways to cut waste never seize. I keep finding more convenient locations for Relocation or a quick pitstop-gas-coffee-cleaning all the time and keep a small notebook in a car with various notes, mileage and travel time. Multiply Online Hours by 100, and then divide by Total Hours. This is a percent of time you spend not working. Refreshing, eh?

8.   Divide number of Trips by Total Hours; and divide Money by number of Trips. These ratios are very useful for historical analysis, when you want to look a year back to find out if a particular month or a weekend

was too hectic (too many trips per hour) or too bombastic (large average payoff per trip). There is no way to control or improve Trips per Hour or Dollars per Trip ratios, but they are great for bragging rights: "I can do 6 trips per hour in Villanova, on a 2.5x surge…" Fisherman's tales, he-he.

9.   I also like to record two biggest fares of the day, class of the ride, its origin and destination. This is how I discovered GREEN Zones to begin with, and got the numbers to back it up.

10.   You can set this all up in Excel, but I prefer to keep my records by hand in a notebook. I think that the process of putting a pen to paper, manually dividing numbers in calculator and taking time to do it mindfully brings a better understanding and usefulness to all this mumbo-jumbo.

Now to the point: anybody, anywhere, anytime can make $100/day and $500/week driving for Uber. It's just a matter of how long it takes… otherwise, they haven't read Papa B's book. This is not a lot of money, but I have made twice as much by following my rule-based system. Can you make more than $1000/week in average America? Yes, it's possible, but not by much. Uber is like a rubber balloon – you can't blow it up beyond certain size or something gonna rip. Say, you already working all $20-30 Online Hours on nights and weekends. Then you add $10-20 Online Hours during the day, with few $5-7 Online Hours in-between. Don't forget to add average downtime. What, you want to work morning hours too? Are you a horse?

I don't want to pass judgement on other people's work habits. We are all adults, doing what we have to do, but shit happens and sometimes precludes us from making as much money as we hoped. Don't divide a bear skin before one is caught – you thought there will be enough for new seat covers and floor mats and mittens and a fur collar for your wife, but in reality it is much smaller. However, it is real and achievable and right there. Your bear fur is 500 bucks. Plan accordingly, everything else is a gift.

(No bears got skinned during writing of this book.)

In the beginning of the book I pointed out that payments for 'X'-class sedan should not exceed $300/month. You are making $500 per week. One week pays for your car plus gas for a week of driving and a little reserve for future repair and maintenance. Anything over $500 is gravy. Second week – insurance, phone, EZ-pass, plus gas and stuff – 500 again, juice is yours. The following two weeks are all profit (minus the usual expenses) and Bob's your uncle.

Chapter 7

What about Rule #4?

This rule is so simple and so easy to understand, it seems barely worth mentioning, but it has wider meaning and couple of important exceptions.

Rule #4   Follow Directions

First of all, take Rule #4 at face value and follow directions on your phone. Navigation will take you there one way or another. Of course, there could be a better route, but every time I deviate – there is an accident blocking the road, or the bridge is out, or it's a wrong way one-way street.

Exception A.

**I take Alternate route only if
I know it and traveled on it recently.**

As my wife often says, *the shortest route is the one you are most familiar with.*

I will follow directions to a T, but it may be insufficient at destination. Uber's navigation is notorious for serving inaccurate locations, especially around big buildings. Malls and large office complex address is often pinned to some loading dock in the back, where mail comes in. This is where navigation is pointing at times, but "People are Not Stupid", they know it and often text their exact location, e.g. Mall entrance, certain store or transportation center. Another typical situation is when people request an Uber while sitting on a backyard, drinking beers'. They know where they are, but the map sees them sitting on a parallel street and serves directions that are two right turns away from true destination.

I have this guide: I follow directions to the end, and once I get there – I will look around and figure it out. When I reach a pin on the map and my destination still not clear, then I park up safely first (Rule #1) and call my passenger (Rule #2). Can you see me outside? Can you tell me where you are, so I can come closer to you? Can you confirm your address? Can you tell me the name of the store you are at or what can you see across the street? And continue like this until I have a solution. No need to be nervous. I assure my customers that I will come for them and don't 'Cancel' (Rule #3). The fish is on a hook, all that's left is to reel it in steadily and surely.

I follow Rule #4 from the moment I get a request. Navigation will offer <u>some</u> kind of the road. I usually don't care what it is, unless I want to make a U-turn instead of going around four blocks. Other than that – there is no reason to worry. As my grandfather used to say, *rushing is suitable only for catching fleas.* The rider sees the same time to arrival as I do. This time takes into account distance, traffic conditions as well as adds a couple of minutes of back-up. Clients can monitor my progress in rider's app on their phone.

In other words – go normally and you will get there on time. There is no reason to get there faster – this is not a race. Follow the directed speed limit.

Same thinking applies after I pick up a passenger. The fish is already in the net – proceed to destination. Their app shows the same duration of the trip as mine. It is what it is. If they are late – it's their problem – I am not breaking laws for anybody!

I usually check directions (especially for longer trips) at the first traffic light or whenever I'm not moving. **I like to confirm route preference with the passenger. If they have their own favorite turns – fine, I follow their directions as long as they lead to the same destination, as an <u>Exception B</u>.**

Lyft's map works better.

Some drivers use other maps as a plugin into app or alongside with it. I heard that there are limitations for that too, but I decided early on to stick to app's native map. If there is a payment dispute regarding overcharging based on longer or inefficient route taken, Uber will take driver's side only if driver followed build-in navigation. I never had this problem, because I follow Rule #4. I had received negative feedback regarding navigation, but they didn't claw back any money and I didn't feel any change in my queue standing at all. I guess, everybody is entitled to their own opinion, as long as it costs nothing.

Inefficient directions and defective locations are the biggest complains of all drivers, and rightly so, as it is a key functionality and translates directly into money made and lost. I would like to propose for everybody to chill, and realize how new this amazing technology still is. Think about it – 5 years ago, there was no Uber or any other ride-sharing service. 10 years ago, a phone on which Uber runs, did not exist yet. Imagine how all this will change... tomorrow. Whatever I write about navigational idiosyncrasies today, will be outdated 6 months from now. There is an army of engineers and computer programmers working on this stuff day and night, all around the world. Give kids a chance – they will sort this out.

Furthermore, I would like to propose an idea that we are in a very early stages of Brave New World, in which ride-sharing will become an integral part of everyday life everywhere. I can imagine people paying monthly memberships of less than it costs to own a car. I can envision self-driving cars coming to the fore, I'm buying 5 of them and putting them out to Uber 24x7, while I sit in front of 5 screens, talking to all those nice people at once.

I am expecting many more ride-sharing services to enter marketplace and possibly diminish early pioneers somewhat. I am referring to "Xerox Phenomenon" – although Xerox holds less than 30% of photocopier's market share, we still call all copies "Xerox", even if they made in machines by other manufacturers. Brand becomes a noun or a verb. In the same light, I see a possibility that someday people will "UBER" in Pick-n-Drop or RidePupsik, or whatever ridiculous name they will come up with for clones of this incredible thing.

Future history is obscure from the present, but past history rhymes with this current "UBER" situation. It has all the hallmarks of Great Inventions that changed the World: railroads, telephone and telegraph, early days of internet, Yuri Gagarin, Google and Amazon and even invention of the wheel. Decades from now, they will study this "UBER" episode and wonder – how did people manage to fuck it up so bad? LOL. No, I'm just kidding.

But seriously, there is one connecting theme, one commonality in all these great advancements – a working man, putting his nose to a grindstone day in and day out – The Driver. No matter what they will "UBER" in years from now, whether it's another Toyota Camry or Papa-B-Five-Screen-Rig, there still be The Driver at the helm.

It is The Driver, who carries heavy responsibility for wellbeing of himself and other people.

It is The Driver, who does the work.

It is the Driver, who makes the money.

The Driver is the final arbiter of everything that has to do with his business, in his car and about his passengers.

MAH UBA

One Thursday night, in the beginning of winter, I was hopping around Villanova, driving drunk college kids around. Call comes in from Kelly's, popular joint on Rt30/Lancaster Avenue. Normally there is no place to park there, but at night traffic on Rt30 drops to a trickle and UBER's simply stop in front of the bar, put flashers on and wait for passengers. Even cops are used to it and often direct passing cars around.

The night was COLD. Freezing rain was lashing sideways in a blistering wind onto a long line of youths waiting to get inside, dressed in... nothing. I had to rub my eyes, I thought I was having visions. Girls in beach-tops and sandals, guys in t-shirts and shorts – had the World gone mad? I was shivering just from looking at them.

My passenger was late. I called. She said to wait – she was paying the bill. Situation normal... and I am standing in the middle of Lancaster Avenue. Suddenly my thoughts were interrupted by a knock on a window. Three half-naked girls want to get in the car, even only for a minute, to get warmed up a bit. I didn't have to think. I took them in, just like I hope somebody would take my children if they were stranded somewhere bitter cold... and in shorts. Minutes later heater was cranking on '5', girls were joyfully chirping in the back and I couldn't be happier, until a deranged shadowy figure fell out of the bar and started banging on a hood and roof of my Beloye Taksi.

Drunken ghost was in feisty mood; screaming and shouting: "Get the fuck out of my car! This is not yo' uba', it's my uba'..."

I rolled down a window. Girls fluttered out.

I said: "Lady, this is not your uber or their uber. This is MAH UBA. I decide who stays and who goes, who gets into a warm car and who stays out in the Freezing Fucking Rain. If you calm down, MAH UBA can give you a ride wherever you go."

I wasn't about to take a raging drunk into my car, alone, at night. There is no telling what this kind of a person will do. I have to think of my own safety per Rule #1, as well as Rule #2, which is much trickier with people under influence.

She came to in two shakes of a lamb's tail, had some of my water, we even managed to carry a short and polite conversation. I kept it neutral. I had enough adventures for that day.

Exception C.

I will not follow any directions that contradict my Rules, or require me to break the Law.

This is MAH UBA.

Papa B's Rules

Rule # 1   Safety First

Rule # 2   Courtesy is the Best Policy

Rule # 3   Take All Trips and Do Not Cancel

Rule #4   Follow Directions

Rule #5   I Do Not pick up in RED Zone

And the Governing Law of them all

This is MAH UBA

UBER TALE

Teheran 17

About 20 years ago we had a business in Ambler, Montgomery County. Shortly after grand-opening some gopnik walks in and cheerfully asks: "So, where are you guys from?" I used to try to clarify that I am a non-religious Jew, born in Ukraine when it was still a part of Soviet Union. My native language is Russian. No, Ukraine is not a part of Russia. Yes, Putin is a dictator. No, Russians love America. Yes, THIS IS my home. No, I don't like Russian food. Yes, Golden Gates is the best Russian restaurant in Philadelphia and so on and so forth.

On that day in Ambler I thought this is too much to explain to a simpleton from Pennsylvania country-side and just said: "I am Ukrainian." I don't know if it was my pronunciation, his hearing or lapses in public education, but gopnik went around town telling people that those new guys on a corner are 'Real Iranians'. It took me a better part of a year to convince locals that: "No, I am UKRAI-nian, not IRA-nian... No, it's not the same thing... No, it's not the same part of the World."

On Tuesday, at 11:07 am, for the first time in my life, I met a real IRA-nian.

Man was in a talkative mood, so I quickly disposed of 'Dictator Putin vs Our Democracy' theme he tried to start with me, and went straight for the jugular. I had an important matter to discuss. Although the ride was about 30 minutes long, there was no time to waste since I wanted to give him a little background behind my 'loaded' question.

From what I remember of History taught in school and books I read on my own - Russia always had a warm relationship with Persia, a part of the World represented now by Iran, and not so much with Arab countries further East. Seemingly different cultures of Russian Empire (followed by multi-national Soviet Union) and different monarchies of Persia were connected for centuries by trade, trust or war. So I ask: "How did Iranians see Russians?"

I think he decided there and then to give me a 'loaded' answer, but first the man wanted to provide some background of his own.

Having left Iran for university in America in 1971, he called himself a 'victim of circumstance'. American degree was no good in post-Shah Iran, but their economy was tanking anyway. Plus mobs in the street chanting "Death to Americans" made his American-born wife very 'uncomfortable'. He praised Shah for developing Iranian oil fields and investing 60 billion of revenues into infrastructure and public projects, making Iran one of the leading economies of Arab World. He said: "Life was pretty good. We had cars and electronics, but we had no political freedoms. Now, there are some kinds of freedom, but economy stinks, country is in isolation, while government squandered 1 Trillion dollars of oil profits."

I was getting tired of his social-economic excursion, when he finally got to the point. In a peculiar Eastern way, there are always two sides to a coin. While Iranian government propaganda in mid-20th Century was highly negative of Russia, Iranian people had great affinity towards Russian culture. His family often enjoyed 'pirozhki' and 'babka', and everything 'Russian' was really cool.

Fast-forward 50 years - Iran is bashing everything American, but people walking around in Levi's jeans, Apple iPhone is 'it' and the best present for a teen-age boy is a NY Yankees baseball hat.

Go figure. East is tricky.

The man spoke with such warmth about his country, I guess that given the choice again he would never gone to America in a first place. The fate of a person is not written on his forehead. It's really all quite random, you know, except...

I told him: "Picking between 'here' and 'there' - I personally choose 'here' every day of the week and twice on a weekend".

I went back to the old country once. After living in America for many years and gotten used to comforts of modern society - it was a fucking nightmare.

"Have you gone back to your lands since then?"- I asked.

"Sure. I go every year if I can and more often while my parents were alive."

I was dumbfounded.

"Wasn't it the place where people from America feel 'UN-comfortable'?", I confronted him.

"O, I couldn't live or work there, but to visit for a couple of weeks is fine. Nobody cares. Traveling in Arab World is not like in Western countries. People move around all the time."

His parents came to Iran from what used to be Azerbaijan. Some family members moved to what is now called Armenia. Borderlines are largely a recent phenomenon and they keep on changing. Just to see your family may require visits to several countries on a same trip.

That was it. A Fat Pitch! We stopped on a red light. I looked him square in the eyes:

"Where is Your Home?"

Iranian didn't have to think.

"HERE. My children and grand-kids are Here. My wife... My life... You know, when I travel There, I can stay for a week, two weeks, but every day after that is like torture. I just want to go home..."

He went quiet and looked out the window. Wrinkled olive skin of his relaxed face basked in diffused sunlight of a cloudy summer noon. We drove in silence through spectacular slopes of Manayunk to where serene waters of Schuylkill River meet Twin Bridge.

Real Iranian looked perfectly comfortable in a back seat of Beloye Taksi.

In a way, All PeopleS are the Same...